For Kedra

CHASED BY TRAUMA

While Running Into Paths of Healing

Blessings & Love, Peace + Healing

Roxie Dewitt Dawson

*Love,
Roxie
6-24-25*

Chased By Trauma....While Running Into Paths of Healing
Copyright © 2025 by Roxie Dewitt Dawson
Published in the USA by Booked Up Publishers

All rights reserved. No part of this book may be reproduced, duplicated, stored in a retrieval system or transmitted in any form or by any means—electronic, mechanical, photocopy, recording, scanning, or other—except for brief quotations, etc. without the prior written permission from the author or appointed designee.

This book was written by the author for educational/informational purposes only. The publisher/author are not rendering any form of legal or professional mental health advice and if such assistance is required, the services of competent, qualified professionals should be sought.

The author has not knowingly engaged in any type of plagiarism or used any individual's original work without either permission or providing proper credit.

Under no circumstances will any legal responsibility be against the author or printers/publishers, for any damages due to the information within this book, either directly or indirectly.

Unless otherwise noted, Scripture quotations are from the Holy Bible, New International Version®, NIV®, Copyright©1973, 1978, 1984, 2011 by Biblica, Inc® Used by permission of Zondervan. All rights reserved worldwide.
www.Zondervan.com. The "NIV" and "New International Version" are trademarks registered in the United States Patent and Trademark Office by Biblica, Inc.®

Scripture quotations marked NKJV are taken from the New King James Version®. Copyright©1982 by Thomas Nelson. Used by permission. All rights reserved.

New Living Translation copyright© 1996, 2004, 2007 by Tyndall House Foundation. Used by permission of Tyndale House Publishers, Inc., Carol Stream, IL 60188. All rights reserved. New Living, NLT, and the New Living Translation logo are registered trademarks of Tyndale House Publishers.

Library of Congress Cataloging-in-Publications Data

Name: Dewitt Dawson, Roxie, author
ISBN: 978-0-9716322-2-6

DEDICATION

I dedicate this book to my two sons (my babies), Erran and Darius "DJ", Erran, our firstborn, and DJ, the youngest of our three sons and our "Baby Boy!" I still feel such deep pain from your deaths and cannot believe that I can no longer hug and hold you. That gnawing feeling hits the bottom of my stomach ever so often and I feel so deeply saddened as a mother. The sweet memories that we made in our short time together is what continues to give me the strength to keep going. "Ain't No Mountain High Enough—Ain't No Valley Low Enough"—to keep our hearts apart! Mommy loves you.

SPECIAL DEDICATION

I dedicate this book to one of the most courageous people alive, Isabella Strahan, who has managed to look the enemy of trauma right smack in the face and say, "Shoot your best shot because I am a powerful rebounder!" Isabella has shown all of us that trauma may come, but it cannot stay.... especially when it has trespassed and is residing illegally! Keep soaring, Isabella. You're definitely an eagle!

GRATITUDE

I will be forever grateful to my Creator...God and to my parents. There would be no me without you! To my middle son, you are the gift that has kept on giving! Thank you for always having my back. God knew how much I would need you to get through the hard times! I love you beyond the moon and the stars! To my sweet baby girl, Sarah. You came into my life at just the right time. God used you to fill those empty places with love, smiles and hugs! You helped me to grow in ways that I did not think were possible! To my incredibly sweet daughter-in-law, you are the best wife and mother in the entire universe! You have been a tremendous blessing to our family from the very beginning. Thank you! Finally, to my husband, thank you for supporting me and allowing me to do what I feel I was created to do! Life hit us real hard, but every lesson was worth the legacy that we will leave our "Seed"...they will always get back up, shake it off and keep moving forward!

CONTENTS

Introduction 9

CHAPTER [1]
Trauma Looks Different on Everyone 19

CHAPTER [2]
Childhood Trauma 37

CHAPTER [3]
Adult Trauma: When Trauma Appears to Be Chasing You 53

CHAPTER [4]
Relationship Trauma 67

CHAPTER [5]
Socioeconomic & Financial/Poverty Trauma 85

CHAPTER [6]
Understanding Intergenerational Trauma 97

CHAPTER [7]
Spiritual Trauma a/k/a "Church Hurt" When the Blessing…
Breaks Us! 109

CHAPTER [8]
How Grief, Trauma, and Emotional Pain are Connected 123

CHAPTER [9]
The Pandemic of 2020 & How Trauma Manifested 139

CHAPTER [10]
Womb Trauma: The Seed of Trauma 151

CHAPTER [11]
    Trauma in the Workplace 161

CHAPTER [12]
    Choosing Healing: Getting Help and Getting Whole! 177

APPENDIX ONE
    Trauma Treatment & Resources 187

Acknowledgments 191
Trauma Quotes by Roxie 195
Notes 197
About The Author 199

"Until you heal the wounds of your past, you are going to bleed. You can bandage the bleeding with food, with alcohol, with drugs, with work, with cigarettes or cigars, with sex, but eventually, it will all ooze through and stain your life. You must find the strength to open the wounds. Stick your hands inside pull out the core of the pain that is holding you in your past, the memories and make peace with them."
—Iyanla Vanzant

"Trauma is not just an event that took place sometime in the past; it is also the imprint left by that experience on mind, brain, and body."
—Bessel van der Kolk, author of *The Body Keeps the Score*

"God will not fix what we will not confront!" Healing from trauma will require us to go inward to the deep, deep places where pain, heartache and emotional wounding has resided; Go there! Sit in every emotion, acknowledge them and then find the courage to HEAL!"
—Roxie Dewitt Dawson

INTRODUCTION

There is another "Silent Killer" among us and it is not hypertension/high blood pressure, heart disease, carbon monoxide poisoning or any other health condition—it's "Trauma!" The impact of trauma is profound and far-reaching and can manifest in ways unthinkable, to include, but certainly not limited to, anxiety, depression, triggers, emotional numbness, dissociation, chronic illness and a myriad of other trauma responses. Trauma is NOT my friend, and it is not yours either! Currently, trauma is at an all-time high. It's a social issue that needs to be addressed and it demands our undivided attention.

Trauma has invaded our homes, our jobs, our worlds and wreaked havoc on our children, our marriages, our families and our lives! It destroys everything in its path! By the time we realize that it's present, nothing is recognizable, and the clean-up may take years…maybe even a lifetime!

Most try to avoid dealing with their trauma, which can be connected to their grief, deep hurt or pain or some other form of emotional wounding. They try to cover their trauma up by working excessively, drinking excessively, shopping excessively and a slew of other addictions and vices that only makes things worse instead of better! I did not do these things to cover up my trauma, but what I did was still not helpful.

What was it that I did? *Nothing.*

Yes, I did nothing about the layers of unhealed trauma that had invaded my life for over thirty-plus years! By the time I realized I had allowed years of anger outbursts, anxiety attacks, bouts of depression, times of extreme distancing and more to steal precious time away from me and my family…the damage was already done and some of it was unrepairable!

Trauma paralyzed my pain. You may ask, "How is this remotely possible?" When the body and brain senses trauma, they naturally activate the "fight, flight, or freeze" response, and the "freeze" can manifest as a state of immobility and cause the body to essentially shut down. Trauma can paralyze pain by triggering the "freeze" response in the body's nervous system, which eventually causes a dissociation from physical sensations, to include emotional pain. This is somewhat of a survival mechanism when the body senses an overwhelming threat; this can and does cause some sort of disruption of our neural pathways to the brain. It makes perceiving and processing sensory information, including pain signals, difficult during a traumatic event.

This is why I say that "trauma stole many years from me" because the trauma was coming so fast and from so many directions that I did not have time to process one thing before I was hit with something else! The many layers of pain that began to build up left me feeling overwhelmed and in a state of not knowing exactly what to do.

There is no doubt that people are experiencing trauma on some level even as I write about it. There are so many people living with residual trauma from childhood or from something that happened during their adult years. Their bodies and brains live in a constant state of vigilance in wait of the next attack or life altering event. Trauma clearly has a severe impact on us because of the way it affects and, ultimately, rewires the brain. Ironically, when the brain goes into stress or gets stuck in stress, it leads to physical symptoms and body changes. These body changes may show up as chronic illness!

INTRODUCTION

Sadly, the number one way most people are treating their trauma wounds is by "Avoidance!" They feel that as long as their old trauma is not upsetting their lives *too much*, then why go to therapy? Why begin conversations that might bring up deep, hurtful feelings, emotional pain and triggers? It's human nature to want to only do things that we see the value in doing.

Some have asked, "Why would anyone want to talk or write about trauma and relive some of the triggers/responses that comes with this?" The answer is simple—I am trying to help countless others to realize how *TRAUMA* disrupts and damages our lives in unimaginable ways! Some of us have seen this in our lives repeatedly, but we do not want to acknowledge that trauma is the culprit. We ride the waves of craziness until the next episode occurs.

I have seen and felt the devastation of trauma and urge people to take their trauma healing more seriously!

I am writing this book and becoming incredibly vulnerable in order to help others learn a little more about "trauma" and the devastating effects it can have on our lives, our marriages and our families.

It is my prayer that by opening up my wounds (some healed and some still healing…) that I will say something that will make someone stop and examine their life to see if trauma has played an "uninvited" role in tearing down their home, their marriage, their families and their relationships! It's so much smarter to get help now versus later.

My experiences with trauma have been unbelievably life-altering, and I feel compelled to share what I have learned, both on a personal and professional level. I am hopeful that by sharing, many will begin to look a little closer at their lives and ask, "Is the trauma that I am holding onto worth the space and damage that it is costing me?"

In other words, you may consider your life to be pretty peaceful right now and would rather not deal with the bouts of anger, the triggers, the insecurity, the confusion, the doubt and so much more that is more than likely a result of "unhealed trauma." Just imagine though, how much healthier your life might be after finally processing past hurt and childhood trauma that has never been addressed.

While I certainly experienced trauma as child, my first deeply traumatizing event happened in August 1987. I had just returned to the United States after living in Germany for three years while my husband served as an active-duty Army Service Member. I did not come back to the "States" the entire time, so I was excited about being back at home around family and friends that I could relate to!

It was because of this deep feeling of wanting to bond with family again that I allowed my firstborn child, our four-year-old son, to visit my parents for one week without me. He had NEVER been out of my sight for more than ten minutes prior to this, but I thought, "What better and safer place besides a grandparents' home?"

Safety is and should always be every parent's first concern when allowing their children to visit other people's homes! While I felt that my baby boy would be safe, it had never crossed my mind to ask if there were any weapons in the home or if they were being stored and locked up properly. Most would not ask when it's a grandparent's home!

So exactly one week after dropping off my little buddy, I got the call every parent prays they'll never get...that my son had died! I got that call mere hours before I was due to pick my "Little Buddy" up! Now when I look back, this event was the real beginning of what has seemed like a lifetime of trauma chasing me.... yet I have continued to run into paths of healing!

Some of these paths looked quite different from others. Some of the paths led me to sitting on the beach staring into space for hours at a time! Some paths of healing were sitting in the whirlpool at the spa in total solace. One path led me to a beautiful park with several

INTRODUCTION

beautiful waterfalls and the soothing sound of the water felt cleansing to my deep emotional wounds that had started to harden and crumble!

As much as I would like to completely forget the details of the day that my first child died…I cannot! I have never screamed louder in my entire life as I did when I was told that my young six-year-old nephew had accidentally shot my baby boy while playing hide-and-seek. It has been over thirty-plus years, but the heartache and trauma from the death of my firstborn has never left me and from what I now know about trauma—it never will!

During the early years of trauma healing after the death of my first child, I was reminded almost daily of a scripture that mentioned both "paths" and "hope," both of which I needed desperately!

The scripture is Psalms 25:4-5 "Show me your ways, LORD, teach me your paths. Guide me in your truth and teach me, for you are God my Savior, and my hope is in you all day long." (NIV)

Now, fast forward thirty-three years to when I was finally feeling healed emotionally and felt the majority of the deep wounds from years of trauma healing were finally looking healthy—the unimaginable happened again!

On September 5th, 2020, another son died in a tragic car accident right down the street from our home. My rainbow baby, the youngest of our three sons and my sweet baby boy who would drive hours just to come and give his mama a hug, was gone!

How could this be? No parent should even experience burying one child—not to mention two! Why would fate deal such a cruel, painful blow to our family? I braced myself because right away I could sense the heaviness of both tragedies weighing heavy on my heart. The compounding stress and trauma was present all over again. The overwhelming days of sadness and tears had returned.

I searched desperately for paths that would lead me to healing only to find out that no such path existed at the time! It was going to take my doing some "inside work" emotionally to even begin to heal enough to keep going as a mother and as a wife, both of which were demanding jobs and require me to be fully present emotionally!

Sometimes, those paths were mini getaways. Other times these paths looked like counseling sessions, brief sabbaticals or nights of walking on the beach alone and praying to God for just a brief answer as to WHY he chose this journey of suffering for me, why I was chosen to play a character in such a traumatizing story.

Nevertheless, I have gathered the pieces of my fragmented heart and want to share very openly and honestly in this book so that someone's life will be blessed and more importantly, healed!

When trauma begins to show up in our lives, we must not adopt an "ostrich mentality" where we put our head in the sand and pretend like nothing has happened or that our pain and wounding does not exist.

I can assure you that trauma does not just magically "disappear" because we do not acknowledge it. On the contrary, the problem gets bigger and bigger until finally "the hurricane" makes landfall and deals a blow that will be evident for what could possibly be generations!

After the tragic deaths of my two sons, I witnessed the devastating effects trauma left on me and my family. I felt so defenseless. I did not think it was possible to heal from so much emotional and mental damage. I kept looking for paths that would ignite healing in my body, mind, soul and spirit. Unfortunately, most of the paths only helped momentarily. I knew that my trauma was complicated. It would take more than a few sessions with a therapist….it would take years! It would take some deep-diving and deep excavation to get to the root of the issues.

Many have asked how I have been able to function and keep going. I always share that my faith in God and the proof that I know

INTRODUCTION

personally how "low" emotionally I had gotten from having to bury a child and the fact that I am now able to share about my experience without being emotionally distraught is evidence that some sort of healing has taken place. The other thing I share is we (humans) do not have too many options when things happen to us that are out of our control. We either "quit" or keep moving!

Have I been able to function and keep going? Most certainly. And, I have even been able to care for a four-month-old baby girl who "appeared" in my life in July of 2013. I was fifty-one years old, and both of our sons had graduated from college. I had no plans of raising any more children, unless they were grandchildren! God obviously loves to rewrite stories because I felt a little like Sarah and Abraham in the Bible who were incredibly old as well when God instructed them that they would become parents.

The real irony of this story though is my daughter's biological father is the nephew who accidentally killed our four-year-old. So theoretically and factually, I am raising the child of the person who accidentally killed my child! Now how is that for an unbelievable story line and maybe even a number one bestseller movie! You can read more about this incredible story by purchasing my first book, *"Silenced By Arms…Children Are Dying."*

So, it is possible **to not be fully healed** from trauma and traumatic events **and to keep moving** until a *TRIGGER* or trauma response stops you right in your tracks!!

The tragic, sudden death of one child is enough to make a parent want to give up on life. The fact that I have experienced this now twice as a mother feels cruel and inhumane. Just pondering over the days, months and years it took to heal enough to survive after the death of the first child was overwhelming all by itself!

Dealing with this kind of complex trauma that has multiple layers of wounding is another reason why I wrote this book. Somebody needs to hear that surviving this level of trauma is possible when we choose to do the work of soul healing.

I am unsure if there is such a thing as "total healing." How does a parent "totally heal" after burying two of their children? The trauma of two of my children dying was not only compounding, but it felt like a nightmarish dream that I did not want to relive. To this day, my mind still poses the question, "How could a loving, caring God allow such a thing to happen to our family?" That one question is still full of the unknown, even as I write these pages.

As I shared earlier, no one in their right mind would choose to write a book like this unless they really wanted to help others! I have seen in my sixty-plus years of life quite the opposite; most people keep their trauma stories to themselves! Some of this is due to shame, some is pride and some could be the mere fact people consider their trauma journey to be deeply personal, and it is! However, there is no need to feel ashamed because none of us asked to be inflicted by trauma and as long as we do not share our stories, we give "shame" that much more power! By sharing our trauma healing stories, we win…we win BIG! There are people out there who really need to hear our stories.

Our society has sold the lie to the masses that as long as you show everyone your "good side" and keep putting bandages over the visible wounds, then no one will know about your invisible childhood trauma wounds, your relationship trauma, your financial trauma and—God forbid—your spiritual trauma or church hurt or any of the other types of trauma wounds!

Please understand that trauma is quite common, and many people have dealt with or may be currently dealing with it. Trauma can have long-lasting effects on your mental and physical health, which is why we must heal! No one gets "extra-credit" for not dealing with their trauma. The wounds are *REAL* and must *HEAL*!!

INTRODUCTION

I am deciding to share my experiences of deep trauma so that someone will have the courage to choose *HEALING* over *HIDING* and *BREAKTROUGH* over *BONDAGE*! Because as long as there is bondage, freedom is nonexistent! It is my eternal prayer that you will choose freedom!

From my "healed heart" to yours,

Roxie

CHAPTER [1]
Trauma Looks Different on Everyone

Going to pick out a casket for my four-year-old baby boy, my firstborn was beyond devastating! As a twenty-five-year-old mother, how was I supposed to go on? How could I even function in order to care for our remaining eight-month-old son who needed me to survive?

Slipping into a deep, dark depression was not even an option. He needed me to heal as fast as possible, so that he would survive! Imagine trying to heal from the devastation and trauma of your child dying suddenly, tragically in your parents' bedroom…while the grief and deep pain that I awoke to every single day was trying to suck me into some dark hole similar to what quicksand does!

It would take ten years for me to finally accept what had happened to our family. During that time, I functioned unknowingly without any professional counseling. I was in such a fragile, confused and broken state! I walked around emotionally numb and traumatized beyond recognition for years!

God knew I still believed in Him but that I also had no interest in having a close, personal relationship with Him at this particular time, because I felt that he could have saved and protected my baby, but he chose not to! I simply could not understand how such a "loving, caring" God who placed the stars and the moon in the sky could allow me to become so broken, so very wounded emotionally!

I believe that everyone's life has a theme! I am uncertain as to why mine is centered around "Trauma."

I have often questioned why some people go through life with hardly anything tragic happening to them and then there are the others (like me) who seem to have been given an extra dose. An even more intriguing question is: "Is this even fair?" What does "fair" even look like? Do we have some hidden super-power of perseverance that illuminates and makes us some sort of target, or maybe it's because God does know who he can trust with the pain, the trauma and the testimony of how we never thought that healing was possible.

This book was difficult to write. Why? Because who wants to write about a subject like trauma? Who wants to relive the sadness, deep pain and emotional roller coaster that is the result of unrelenting trauma in their life?

Even with the heaviness that came with writing this book, the more the distractions and discouragement came, I still knew that it was something I had to complete. I knew that although I experienced some hard moments emotionally, God had equipped me for this assignment and that His grace would enable me to complete what "He" had started!

Trauma is such a huge conversation piece currently in our society. Why wouldn't it be though? Our society seems to be a trauma-ridden with traces of trauma on almost every corner. Trauma seems to be the least common denominator in every equation with results showing up every single place that we look! Trauma can come in so many forms and affect people in a number of ways.

Prior to writing this book, I was unaware how trauma affects so many. From young children to senior citizens, trauma seems to creep in and makes itself comfortable, while slowly but surely reshaping everything it comes into contact with! Our lives are never the same after a traumatic event. Even if we do not acknowledge that things are different—they are!

So, it is my prayer that this book will make your life better by causing you to take long, hard looks at any areas of your life that's "Unhealed" from unaddressed trauma! I am writing this book because I want people to know that trauma can destroy your life if we do not heal. It's crucial that we HEAL! Future generations in our family are dependent upon us healing from trauma.

Even if you have lived a pretty "cool life" with minimal emotional disruptions from unaddressed trauma…just think how much better it could have been had you looked inward and dealt with that one thing (maybe your bouts of anger) that kept coming back over and over again? What if trauma was behind that life-changing bad decision?

You may be aware of how unhealed/unprocessed trauma has affected your life, but you would rather just leave the past in the past. I get it! Because quite frankly, everyone is not impacted by trauma in the same way. It is possible for an event to be inconvenient, difficult and even stressful, but not necessarily traumatic.

Most of us can recognize things that are keeping us from being all that we were created to be. Every now and then we will peek inside our chaotic worlds and decide that now is not the time to deal with "the issues" or the unhealed trauma. We see what is happening, but we do not want to believe what we are seeing because, quite frankly, it is possible to "Look" at a thing and still not "See" it! More importantly, others normally see things about us that we do not or cannot see ourselves! The effects of trauma will keep showing up no matter how many bandages people try to put over them.

Some people believe that they escaped the scars trauma leaves, but it has been scientifically proven that trauma actually never leaves our bodies…it gets stuck in our bodies, our brains and our nervous system.

Dr. Bessel van der Kolk summarizes over four decades of experience studying the impact of childhood trauma and emotional regulation.

He wrote a book, *The Body Keeps the Score*, to further explain how trauma looks different on everyone and that even people who consider themselves successful or productive in life are still not exempt from the impact of trauma.

I sincerely believe that we are put on this earth to make it better in some way. Our life experiences are not just for us, because if that is the case, how sad! I believe every single thing that happens to us or for us is so we can help someone else. In order to do that, we must heal from trauma because trauma affects our lives and our legacy!

So, whatever you learn as a result of reading this book…please

"Pass It On" so others know that it's important to heal from trauma!

Writing about trauma can get super complicated because there is so much that can be said about trauma and the short and long term effects of it. Trauma really does look different on everyone. That's why so many can hide their scars from childhood trauma and even some adult trauma for their entire lives!

I am writing this book to share my experiences with people who are looking at their "unhealed trauma" every single day but have no idea what is happening!

From the outside, most people look like what society calls "normal." The problem with that stereotypic assumption is that trauma looks different on everyone!

Nearly everyone on the planet will experience some form of trauma in their lifetime—it's just a part of life!

TRAUMA LOOKS DIFFERENT ON EVERYONE

According to the National Council for Behavioral Health[1] (now known as, National Council for Mental Wellbeing) n.d.

- 70% of adults (223.4 million people) in the United States have experienced some type of traumatic event at least once in their lifetime
- 90% of clients in public behavioral health program have experienced trauma
- Trauma is a risk factor in nearly all behavioral health and substance use disorders
- 83% of teens experience a traumatic event in adolescence, and 15% of girls and 6% of boys develop PTSD
- Adults over 65 have the highest trauma rate of any age group

The reason it's important to acknowledge when we have been affected by trauma is because when those traumatic events are not fully processed, they can directly or indirectly harm your physical and emotional health. More and more research is showing how trauma is stored in the body and in your nervous system as an overactive stress response. So many times when doctors can find nothing wrong as far as medical tests go—could it be the stored trauma that's affecting us?

Stored trauma must be released in a healthy way so that it will not have a negative impact on our bodies healing capacity. A big key to releasing trauma is to calm our minds, bodies and spirits enough to feel safe. Feeling safe is one of the most important factors in trauma healing because it will allow us to naturally release stored hurt, pain and emotional baggage. Safety can look differently to different people. Being in a healthy, secure relationship is safety for some.

Examples of trauma could look like:

- *the child who was sexually violated
- *identity bias or violent acts
- *the child being bullied at school everyday
- *the young lady who was sexually violated on a date
- *anger from a bad divorce
- *financial disasters/bankruptcies
- *a major vehicle accident or traumatic death
- *verbal or emotional abuse from a bad relationship
- *the couple who lost their third baby prematurely
- *depression from someone close to you dying
- *loss of a job or sudden homelessness
- *loss of a home by fire or natural disaster
- *the patient who came close to dying from a serious illness
- *the police officer who shot and killed his first perpetrator
- *the student who experienced shouts of racial epithets
- *the elderly person who loses their home after owning it for years
- *the parishioner who thought they were "safe" but was emotionally injured in the church
- *the person who wakes nightly after only three hours of sleep
- *political chaos, world affairs and/or social unrest
- *fear, anxiety and stress from marches, rioting and upheavals
- *trauma has even been associated with "clutter"

There are so many more scenarios that could be added to this list, but the realization is that trauma does not have a specific look. On the contrary, it can appear to look completely "normal." I assure you

TRAUMA LOOKS DIFFERENT ON EVERYONE

trauma does not discriminate. Trauma does not care about how much money is in your bank account or that you live in a five-million-dollar home! Trauma is not interested in your title or your status quo! Absolutely no one is exempt from the blows that trauma delivers!

> Trauma does not care about how much money is in your bank account or that you live in a five-million-dollar home! Trauma is not interested in your title or your status quo!

Many try to hide behind their wealth, their titles, their notoriety and so much more in order to cover up their trauma wounds. I assure you that such a thing is nonexistent. Besides, all that hiding still doesn't get them any closer to healing the childhood wounds that have inflicted eternal pain and damage.

First, let's define the word. What exactly is "trauma?" According to the Oxford Language Dictionary, trauma is a deeply distressing event or disturbing experience. According to *Psychology Today2,* it is a "disturbing event that infringes upon an individual's sense of control and may even reduce their capacity to integrate the situation or circumstances into their current reality."

Trauma is a wound. It's a psychological or emotional response to an event or an experience that is difficult to forget and one that can continue to show up years later when not properly managed or when healing has not taken place. Trauma overwhelms the nervous system and can create fear. Fear of the unknown and fear of how to process the known. It is imperative that people know that healing comes at a great cost, but it will be worth every single minute of healing!

Trauma can be an incredibly stressful and frightening event that is difficult to cope with and hard to manage causing circumstances to become out of our control. The worst part about trauma is the "disconnect" it causes. Many times, when people are saying that are "introverts" or "loners," it could be a trauma response or their way of regulating their emotions.

One of the most important things to realize about trauma is that it causes an emotional WOUND and wounds (both physical or mental) must be attended to! When ignored, they will surely infect other parts of your life to include your spouse, your extended family, your friendships, your work relationships and coworkers and so much more. Unhealed emotional wounds can have a devastating effect on entire families, communities and even generations!

This is exactly how our lives become "toxic," and we run from pillar to post trying to see where the leak is. The sad part is that by the time the "leak" is found, so much damage has been done that it's nearly impossible to repair!

The reason trauma looks different on everyone is because everyone has a different story about trauma or their traumatic experience. Another reason that trauma looks different from person-to-person is because so many people spend the majority of their time trying to cover up their emotional scars!

While we know that physical wounds/scars can be seen, emotional wounds are "invisible." Others might not be able to see them, but we can *feel them*. These emotional wounds need time to heal just like the physical ones do!

When we touch an "unhealed" physical wound, we say, "Ouch!" The same thing happens when we "touch" an "unhealed" emotional wound. This response is called a "trigger" or a trauma response.

TRAUMA LOOKS DIFFERENT ON EVERYONE

While writing this book, my mind began to take me back to the early years of my marriage. I started to think about every single incident in our marriage where I now see the effects of "trauma" caused me to behave in ways and do things that I now cannot believe!

None of it involved illegal drugs or alcohol or any other addictive behavior but the "anger bouts" were definitely at the forefront and would be a go-to trauma response until I had finally had enough and sought support by way of therapy.

> Deciding to heal from trauma is a decision that has to come from the core of your soul.

Deciding to heal from trauma is a decision that has to come from the core of your soul. A person must get "sick and tired" of allowing trauma to disrupt their life and destroy their marriage, family, home and so much more.

Trauma in the United States appears to be at an all-time high! While writing this book, so many traumatic things have happened in our country. I've learned of people being set on fire in the New York subway, a well-known CEO being shot by a former valedictorian, delivery men being killed, violent robberies, cases of abuse and so much more. Even the 2024 presidential election was traumatic for some and had people (including myself) drifting from one emotional high or low to another!

There have been literally thousands of violent events in our country that have left the nation in a state of trauma. Traumatic events happen so often that many have become desensitized and can only handle the mental impact that it causes for brief periods.

Thus, trauma looks different on everyone, and we can never tell what's really going on inside another human being's brain.

Let's examine some of the different classes of trauma, which may help to explain why trauma looks so different on everyone.

Trauma normally falls within one of these three classes:

- Acute Trauma – responses to a one-time event (one example is a car accident or a natural disaster)

- Chronic Trauma – prolonged traumatic events, which can create trust issues in the relationship (examples include bullying, sexual abuse, domestic violence, etc.)

- Complex Trauma – ongoing trauma and normally seen in interpersonal relationships giving a person a feeling or being TRAPPED! This can really be mentally taxing (family of origin drama, childhood abuse, etc.)

Then there is something called Large "T" Trauma and Small "t" trauma. Large "T" trauma is the type that most people think of when they think of trauma. Psychology Today3 defines Large "T" trauma as "an extraordinary and significant event that leaves the individual feeling powerless and possessing little or no control in their environment."

Trauma can stem from mental, emotional, physical or spiritual roots. Sometimes the wounds that we cannot see can hurt us more than the ones we can see and can take longer to heal!

Just living life and going through the accumulation of stressors on a daily basis or what we call "less pronounced events" can also cause trauma. Small "t" traumas are "events that exceed our capacity to cope and cause a disruption in emotional functioning." While such events may not be necessarily life-threatening, they can cause people to feel helpless in their circumstances and many may even begin to feel hopeful.

As I review these definitions, I realize I have experienced trauma in each of these groups at different times in my life. Had I known then what I know now about trauma, I would have taken my treatment and healing more seriously. This is why I am on an all-out mission to get people to take their mental health more seriously. Especially in my race (Blacks/People of Color) because our ancestors experienced trauma in some of the cruelest ways. There could quite possibly be residue of intergenerational trauma in the bloodline. Now is the time to "stand in the gap of healing" for future generations. Now is the time for healing to be manifested!

Our forefathers and great grandparents watched as their spouses, children, grandmothers and grandfathers were dragged away from them at any given moment, day or night. This is beyond traumatic and has affected families throughout generations.

As I look back over my life, every traumatic incidence felt overwhelming. I even remember experiencing physical symptoms that seemingly "popped up" after my second child died tragically.

It had only been nine days since we had laid our youngest son, Darius (our 32-year-old baby boy) to rest when I found myself not wanting to get out of bed to celebrate or even acknowledge that I was turning 59 years old! It may have been my birthday, but what was there to celebrate? At that point, I felt my life had made absolutely no sense. It looked like a bomb had exploded and the pieces were scattered everywhere.

Our immediate family (my husband, my son, daughter and daughter-in-law) had rented an Airbnb in Charleston, South Carolina. We needed some quiet time after being around so many people following Darius' death. We needed time to cry alone without the stares from others and the constant questions of "Are you okay?" I wanted to answer each one with a "Do I look okay?" and "No, I will never be okay in some ways!" and "Would you be after burying your second child?"

During our short sabbatical, everyone was so quiet. It was evident we were definitely grieving and were still in shock as to how things happened so fast! My not wanting to get out of bed would be the beginning of my fight with depression, sadness and hopelessness. Fighting was something that was not new to me!

I knew that I could not afford to "quit" because I had two children in Heaven and two still in the Earth who needed and wanted me to keep going! I remember feeling like an invisible ball and chain was wrapped around my neck. I had little energy and did not have an appetite and had to continuously force myself to eat so my body would not let me down! Trauma attacks our bodies, minds, souls and spirits. It screams so loud that no amount of quietness can exist.

In the months that followed after burying my second child, trauma began to show up in some of the strangest places. I realized trauma really does look different on any given day!

Some days it was very noticeable. Other days, although it was still walking right beside me, no one could see it unless something triggered me. It is those triggers, a scent that reminds us of our loved one, a song that comes on, a movie scene that brings back happy or sad memories—these things can bring a flood of tears at the drop of a dime. Only time will be remedy for certain reactions to some grief.

I remember sitting in a particular restaurant where my son and I would enjoy lunch occasionally and everything seeming pretty calm until the food arrived. I hadn't realized it at the time, but this was my first time ordering since his death. I looked down and saw my son's favorite Chinese foods…fried dumplings. The restaurant was pretty crowded, and everyone seemed to be locked into their own private conversations, but then it happened.

I burst into tears and could not stop crying. I covered my face with every napkin I could find and wanted to run out of the restaurant. When I finally opened my eyes, there were several individuals around me and others looking to see if they could help in any way. This was my new normal and I would have to embrace it!

I assured them that I was okay and that we had just buried our second child. I shared a few details about my son's accident and, as unbelievable as it was, many of them had heard about the accident because it was so horrific!

I managed to take a bite or two of my lunch and then gathered my things and prepared to pay my check when the owner of the restaurant came over. She told me that she was so deeply saddened by the news that I had shared and then informed me that my check was taken care of. I thanked her and exited the building before anyone else could stop me.

I felt awful about having caused such a scene at the restaurant, but I knew that day was the beginning of a healing journey that would have several twists and turns, some of which would be unrecognizable to people who had not experienced the vast amount of trauma and emotional wounding that I had.

The previous scenario in the restaurant is what happens when a traumatic experience brings on a "trigger." A trigger is a stimulus that sets off a memory of a trauma or a specific portion of a traumatic experience4. A trigger can be any sensory reminder of the traumatic event. It could be a particular food or smell, a noise, music, a physical or visual scene or sensation. There are also at least four common responses to trauma, and they are:

> ➢ Fight – Taking action against a threat

- Flight – Fleeing from a threat

- Freeze – A response that develops from the stressful situation

- Fawn – Doing something to soothe or calm someone

Depending on how we use these defense mechanisms will determine whether they will be healthy/helpful or unhealthy and/or further escalate situations.

Our thirty-two-year-old son died only a few miles from where we had lived for years. The area where we live only has two streets that could take us to the main parts of our city, so we were forced to drive by the location where our son died almost daily.

Some days, I would brace myself prior to approaching the site and then other days, I would just break down and cry. This happened for the first year after my son's death and then I noticed that I could go pass the site without breaking down. I really tried not to even leave my house on the anniversary or his death and his birthday.

So how exactly does trauma show up? Does it announce its entrance? Does it send you a notice prior to invading your emotions? How is trauma showing up in your marriage, your life, in your relationships? This is a question that only you can answer.

The sooner you stop and do a self-evaluation to see if you have unhealed trauma or emotional wounds that still need to be healed, the sooner your life will be calmer. And if your health has been affected, you may even see things get much better in this area as well.

Questions for Reflection:

THOUGHTS:
What are your thoughts on how trauma might have affected your life? Has it looked different at different times?

FEELINGS:

What are you feeling in your body or spirit after reading?

BEHAVIOR:

What, if anything, will you change about your life after reading this chapter?

CHAPTER [2]
Childhood Trauma

Growing up in one of the poorest of the one hundred counties in North Carolina was traumatic in and of itself!

Now that I am able to talk about it without breaking down continually, I believe it is the early trauma that can seriously derail our lives. It is now my lifetime goal to shed some light on the seriousness of not healing from childhood trauma and traumatic events. So many studies now are revealing that childhood trauma follows us into adulthood and can entrap us into a lifetime of self-abusive thinking and actions, if not properly processed and treated.

So many young children have become victims of sexual abuse/molestation, emotional, mental, physical and even economical abuse rendered from the hands of an alcoholic or irresponsible parent, acts of violence and so much more. Many of them were even exposed to these life events before the crucial age of four or five years old!

Trauma can be tiring, exhausting to carry! It has a way of shaping us into someone unrecognizable to the people closest to us and, most importantly, to the people who love us the most. Childhood trauma especially needs to be taken more seriously because this is where foundations for life are being built, and if things are damaged at this level, it could quite possibly cause damage for life!

Research has shown that trauma survivors suffer far more illnesses (and I would like to add both physical and mental illness counts here). For example, the Adverse Childhood Experience Study found that "survivors of childhood trauma are 5,000 percent more likely to use drugs, attempt suicide, and suffer eating disorders. Muscle tension, disease, and injury are some of the physical manifestations of this preoccupation."

The Centers for Disease Control and Prevention shared that "childhood trauma is our single largest public health issue—but one that is largely preventable by early prevention and intervention."

According to SAMHSA (Substance Abuse and Mental Health Services Administration), childhood trauma occurs more than we think. More than two thirds of children reported at least one traumatic event by age 16. Some of the events may include:

- Community or school violence (school shootings, bullying, physical threats/physical assaults)
- Psychological, physical, or sexual abuse
- Witnessing or experiencing domestic violence
- Sudden loss or death of a close relative
- National disasters or homes burning down
- Experiencing homelessness
- Military parent deployment
- Serious accidents or a terminal illness

The signs of traumatic stress vary from child to child and may have both short- and long-term effects. Trauma is a risk factor for nearly all behavioral health and substance use disorders. Some signs of unhealed childhood trauma that may be showing up later in life include, but are not limited to:

- ❖ Blaming others for what has happened in your life
- ❖ An excessive amount of negativity
- ❖ Becoming dysregulated very quickly

- ❖ Isolating often and for long periods of time
- ❖ Neglecting your self-care and basic needs consistently
- ❖ Toxic relationships
- ❖ Numbness and out of touch emotionally

The impact of child traumatic stress can and does last well beyond childhood—which is why this problem must be taken seriously. Research continues to show that childhood trauma survivors may experience learning problems/delayed learning, which results in lower grades and an increase in behavioral issues, to include in and out of school suspensions and expulsions.

Children experiencing traumatic stress normally have increased use of government health and mental health services. One of the most serious issues that is normally seen with children who have been exposed to high levels of trauma is long-term health problems, such as childhood obesity, diabetes and heart disease.

I can attest to children having more health issues when exposed to higher levels of stress and trauma. I grew up with six siblings and both parents. All nine of us packed into a small, barely eighteen-hundred-square-feet, three-bedroom home. There were four girls and three boys, and we had three beds total! Do the math…that's seven humans trying to sleep comfortably in three beds! It never panned out, and how could it? LOL! We made it work and survived only by the grace of God!

As a child, I was diagnosed with severe, chronic asthma and this would be the beginning of trauma starting to chase me. I remember having my first serious asthma attack around the young age of five. My parents could not afford to take me to the emergency room in order to get a "breathing treatment" and furthermore, we did not even have a local hospital. The closest hospital was ten minutes away in Loris,

South Carolina, which explained how so many people died before they could even get to the hospital!

The fear and trauma I experienced during my early childhood was definitely from believing that I would die from one of my asthma attacks. I remember balling up in a fetal position during my attacks and just breathing so hard in order to inhale as much air as possible. My parents gave me a tiny yellow pill called "Primatene" that made me start spinning around and around.

This was such a scary experience for a child and all I could do was ride the wave out until the next episode. I found out later in life that side effects from this medicine range from "headaches, nausea, vomiting, nervousness, dizziness, shaking (tremors), trouble sleeping, stomach upset, sweating, dry mouth, coughing, sore throat and more."

I am so blessed to still be alive and I am grateful to Almighty God for healing me from asthma around the age of fourteen or fifteen! The years of trauma from each scary asthma attack is etched in my memory but thankfully, I have been able to get pass the triggers that used to come when I would think about how it affected me.

During the early sixties when I was born, many of our neighbors and family members did not have hot running water/plumbing inside, so we had to "heat" our water on stoves, etc. Many also did not have inside bathrooms, which talk about traumatic, forced us to go outside in what was called an "Outhouse"—not to be confused with the guest houses that are outside some of these million-dollar homes that we see now. It was everything but luxurious!

Ours was a small, self-made wooden shed-like contraption that was dark, musky smelling and even had a big dark hole similar to the modern-day toilet seats but certainly nowhere near as nice! Experiencing things like this is enough to scar a child mentally or emotionally for life. Early trauma is even more serious than adult trauma because of the developmental factors involved. Things that happen to us when we are young can literally shape our entire lives. This is why trauma should not be taken lightly.

One of the largest sources of childhood trauma is "traumatic separation" that comes from either parents divorcing or when a child has prolonged separation from a caregiver (which is a break in their attachment bond that can have fatal consequences to say the least).

Writing this book has really been an eye-opener and I am beginning to understand why we have so many social issues in our country and how many of them are centered around violence and mental health issues. We appear to have gotten complacent concerning the importance of addressing and treating child and adult mental health that may have resulted from childhood trauma.

I continue to meet people daily who share traumatic things from their childhood but who have never gone to therapy for it. I met people who could relate to this experience of an "outhouse" who still some fifty/sixty years later did not care to talk about it! Unfortunately, instead of opening up and talking about their childhood trauma, most choose to forget it and just pretend as if it did not happen.

Again, if they just look back over their life, they will see where some of the unhealed childhood trauma affected some of their personal relationships. A child with a complex trauma history may have problems in their future romantic relationships, in friendships, and even with authority figures, such as teachers, police officers, employers and judges.

I am hoping that by sharing openly about my trauma journey this will provoke conversation amongst all ages and cultures. Because the reality is nearly everyone will face some form of trauma in their lifetime. The most important thing to realize is when those traumatic events are not fully processed, they can harm both your physical and emotional health.

In later chapters, we will take a deep dive into how trauma is stored in the body in our nervous systems as an overactive stress response. One of the keys to releasing trauma in our body is to calm the mind and body enough to feel safe. Feeling safe is crucial in releasing the negative emotional baggage.

Upon writing this book, I started thinking about how trauma had affected my childhood. Although I will discuss it in a later chapter on socioeconomic and financial, being raised in an underserved, economically poor community where blacks lived in one area of this small rural town and the whites lives in another was a setup for a childhood history of trauma. Although I now know better, it seemed like the white families lived in the nicer, bigger homes.

So early on, I understood that being poor was definitely traumatic and could have a significant impact on how successful I could be, if I allowed it to define me. I tucked those thoughts as far back in my mind as I could and just concentrated on doing my very best in school.

I was born and raised in a small rural town called Tabor City, North Carolina, which is in the southeastern part of the state and about thirty minutes north of Myrtle Beach, South Carolina. According to the 2020 U.S. Census, Tabor City had a population of approximately thirty-eight thousand people.

Growing up in a fairly poor rural community has given me more firsthand knowledge when speaking about childhood trauma. I just believe that it is almost impossible to write or speak about things that you have not experienced. Having older siblings was such a gift though because they shielded us (the last two of the seven) from so much. They protected us from lots of things that could have been traumatic or at least caused some anxiety due to our circumstances.

While having a chronic illness was part of my childhood trauma story, I experienced other forms of trauma as well. As a result of living near huge, wooded lots and even a "canal ditch," I would see snakes almost on a daily basis. This more than likely explains my being petrified of snakes to this day. I am probably one of the most courageous humans you will meet until I see a snake.

My younger sister and I would go over to this older lady's home almost daily. Her name was Ms. Oree. She was known for selling bootlegged (illegal) alcohol or moonshine. I'm not sure what they called it, but I know my sister and I witnessed lots of older men and some women being intoxicated on a daily basis. Most of it was not scarring, but there were times when arguments would break out between two intoxicated men or sometimes even between Ms. Oree and one of her customers. It would be calm until one of them made her angry and then she would start throwing items and breaking/busting up anything that she could grab. This unhealthy seed may have been planted in my life from seeing this because early in my marriage, I had a habit of throwing things when I got upset as well. Again, trauma leaves an imprint either in the brain or in the body.

My cure for this came when I busted up something really sentimental and valuable and that was the turning point for me. I refused to waste money like that and was tired of being enraged and out of control emotionally as well!

One of the most traumatic things that I experienced as a child was when I almost ran into a long black snake while running through the path to Ms. Oree's house. This memory has never left my mind or my nervous system for that matter.

Anyway, we would run super fast through this wooden path when going to Ms. Oree's house because we feared seeing or stepping on a snake. There were all types of snakes near our home. I have seen black snakes, green snakes, red and brown snakes and maybe even white snakes. There were rattlesnakes and even water moccasins and Lord knows what else. I am almost getting triggered as I write this.

I have other stories of childhood trauma that although they do not prevent me from functioning as a healthy, normal adult, they may be the reason behind some of my decisions as an adult.

For example, as much as I love to grow my own fresh vegetables, when I think about the snakes that I saw when going out behind our home to pick a few cucumbers from our family garden, I simply refuse to have one as an adult. I have even thought about having a fresh herb garden with a wooden box around it in my backyard, but again, the thought of going back there and possibly seeing a snake just sends chills down my back!

I am sharing these examples of how childhood trauma may be the root cause of some of our adult personality issues, and while they do not have to be disabling, they certainly are still stored someplace in the body, brain or nervous system!

Another funny story from my childhood was when I fell from a homemade swing and all the children laughed hysterically. My older brothers had assisted us in building a swing in our backyard. The tree that was used was huge and had strong, healthy-looking limbs. It took hours (almost the entire day) to construct this child masterpiece. I was known as a young leader even as a child and so I was determined to go first. Well, no one argued because I really think they knew that the safety of this contraption was extremely unreliable. LOL!

So after everyone gathered around, I preceded to hop up on this dangerous looking swing. At first it felt like the one on the school playground, but it was everything but that. The one at the school had thick, heavy metal chains and ours had some old, worn heavy-duty rope. Anyway, I begin to sing, "Tie a Yellow Ribbon Round the Ole Oak Tree" and after about a minute of singing it happened! The rope broke and there I went. Bottom first to hit the ground and then the remainder of my body succumbed to this playground tragedy. The kids could not stop laughing. I began to cry, more from embarrassment/emotional injury than a bodily injury.

Again, the way I can recount the intricate details of this day that happened over 50 years ago is evidence that *The Body Keeps the Score1* just as Dr. Bessel van der Kolk has stated. Dr. van der Kolk's work for over forty years validates how trauma has a different impact at different stages of development and that disruptions in care-giving systems have additional effects.

There has been so much research done regarding childhood trauma and its effects, but one particular book was extremely helpful in bringing about clarity in this area. In *"What Happened to You?" Conversations on Trauma, and Healing* (Perry and Winfrey, 2021)[2] the authors state that "nearly 40 percent of children under the age of eighteen have suffered some sort of trauma." They go on to share a recent study by the National Survey of Children's Health found that almost 50 percent of the children in the United States have had at least one significant traumatic experience.

The thing that I love most about Oprah's and Dr. Perry's research is that it explains the importance of not just concentrating on "What's wrong with you?" It shifts to the more important dialogue of "What happened to you?" Dr. Perry explains in the book why understanding how the brain reacts to stress or early trauma helps clarify how what has happened to us in the past shapes who we are.

This particular book clarified so much about trauma for me and why there has been a shift in perspective that honors the "power of the past to shape our current functioning."

Again, the fundamental question is no longer "What's wrong with you," but rather "What happened to you?"

While writing this book, I spoke with individuals who had experienced severe childhood trauma and had never really received the proper therapeutic treatment for it. One case in particular was a male in his late forties who shared how when he was around ten or eleven years of age, he witnessed a close male relative around the same age being sexually assaulted by some boy cousins.

While he expressed gratitude that they did not attack him, he expressed how very traumatizing it was. He went on to share how it affected his life and how he now realizes where the root cause of years of sexual addiction, promiscuity and an out-of-control lifestyle was probably the result of this traumatizing event. The psychological and emotional trauma that followed him into adulthood originated from untreated childhood trauma.

Even his intimate relationships with the opposite sex had been greatly affected and he was extremely remorseful for having injured so many women emotionally and otherwise. Unfortunately, the damage had been done, but at least he understood where the "root cause" stemmed from. The good news about this case is that he was able to begin much needed trauma healing and can now have healthier and happier relationships in the future!

This is only one example of how childhood trauma can follow us and affect our lives as adults. I also have met numerous women who were sexually assaulted or had been molested as a child. Most of them admitted that they never really healed from the past trauma, and they also noticed how it had affected so many of their adult relationships.

I could give hundreds more examples where childhood trauma is a powerful antecedent and determinant for future adult behavior. This is why I am writing this book and sharing my story in hope of convincing many to stop and heal from trauma whether it's from our childhood or from our adult years.

Finding the courage to confront the issues in order to live healthy, whole lives is really the only thing that matters. No one can do trauma healing for us though—it's an inside job!

CHILDHOOD TRAUMA

As an educator, I think about the thousands of children who attend school every day after witnessing something traumatic the night before. These children are expected to come and perform "on task" in a demanding learning environment. Unless they feel safe enough to share with their teachers or an adult who they trust, no one will every know about the vast amount of emotional baggage they are carrying.

I sincerely believe that we are letting our children in this country down when it comes to their mental health and trauma healing. I am almost certain the majority of behavioral problems we see in the classroom can be traced back to a traumatic event of a mental health crisis that has left the child unable to regulate on his/her own.

> Finding the courage to confront the issues in order to live healthy, whole lives is really the only thing that matters. No one can do trauma healing for us though—it's an inside job!

I personally do not believe that our government is doing enough to combat the effects of childhood trauma. I do not want to elaborate on this too much though because I am not privileged to information surrounding funding and programs to help alleviate the effects of childhood trauma.

Bringing about more attention to and acquiring more funding for victims of childhood trauma is certainly one of my forever lifetime goals now, and I do plan to advocate for additional funding in this area because I believe deeply in the seriousness of this endeavor!

My heart aches when I think about the millions of children who go to school every single day after a night of adults shouting, using profanity, being angry and having outbursts! This type of aggravated assault on their bodies, minds, souls and spirits is why some of our youth are not thriving! It could quite possibly be the reason why there is so much youth violence in school and in the community. Could it be that the unhealed trauma that these children are carrying is weighing them down at a level that is simply unimaginable?

Questions for Reflection:

THOUGHTS:

What are your thoughts about any childhood trauma you may have experienced after reading this chapter?

FEELINGS:

What are you feeling in your body or spirit after reading this chapter about childhood trauma?

BEHAVIOR:

How did any childhood trauma that you experienced contribute to some of your adult behavior?

CHAPTER [3]
Adult Trauma: When Trauma Appears to Be Chasing You

Imagine running as fast and as hard as you possibly can in order to get away from a force that has hit you several times before and crushed the very life out of your soul! By the time you realize what is happening to you, months and even years evaporate right in front of your very eyes! You begin to question how things got out of control so fast. What made you so angry for so long? And why didn't you have the courage to ask for help and confront this monster that steals years of life from you and your loved ones?

This enemy causes even the best and the strongest to dwindle under its power. Imagine running for days, for years but this "unfriendly force" always seems to catch you and packs a deadly sucker punch like nothing else has or will. It appears that the majority of us have had a few run-ins with this unfriendly force called "Trauma!"

> Trauma has a way of creeping up on you when you least expect. Trauma has a mind of its own. Trauma has its own timeline and its own path.

Although I had been affected by trauma as a young girl, I did not know that it would follow me on my life's journey. I thought that it would eventually find someone else to harass in the way that it had harassed me. Knowing what I know now about trauma, I realize that it has invaded the lives of thousands, millions of people who have been hit, but seem to still go about their lives as if nothing happened… until something actually happens!

Trauma has a way of creeping up on you when you least expect. Trauma has a mind of its own. Trauma has its own timeline and its own path. Trauma does not discriminate at all. No one gets to dictate when it will strike next. No one gets to decide how long it will stick around. The impact of trauma sometimes will not be visible for years and leaves most of us with only two choices….either to keep going or to quit! Healing from trauma is a personal journey and it is not linear.

After burying two of my three sons, I experienced trauma at a level that I pray no one else ever does. As a result of these life altering events, I knew that I had to write this book. I believe that God Almighty has equipped and kept me so that I can share this miracle of survival from unrelenting trauma for over thirty-plus years!

As I sat on the beach with my husband, our young daughter played and laughed continually. It was the perfect time to be on the beach as the beautiful yellowish-orange sun began to fade in the sunset. We commented how peaceful and serene things had finally become after experiencing the trauma that had ensued from the pandemic earlier in the year. Like so many others, we had waited and waited to venture out due to the fear of catching the deathly Covid virus and ending up in a hospital or worse…the morgue!

The short two-day getaway almost did not happen because our youngest son Darius seemed a bit disturbed about something prior to our leaving, but he reassured us that he would be fine.

My mother instinct within me would not let me accept his response though, and something began to make me feel unsettled. I almost told my husband that maybe we should cancel the trip so we could see if Darius needed medical attention. I've always been an "overthinker"

ADULT TRAUMA: WHEN TRAUMA APPEARS TO BE CHASING YOU

and sometimes will worry about my children's safety nonstop. I actually believe this is a maternal trait and something that numerous mothers can probably relate to.

I remember sitting on the beach that day thinking how peaceful and soothing it all felt. I even mentioned to my husband that "this is the life that God had planned for us" and that we needed to embrace it and be intentional about getting away and getting in our quiet spaces. Little did I know that within 24 hours, our lives would be turned upside down again.

I can still remember my husband and young daughter coming back from the hotel pool and the frightening expression on my husband's face. He looked away as he told me, "We have to go back home immediately...DJ has been in a car accident." The fact that he "looked away" should have alerted me to the seriousness of the matter, but for some reason, it did not.

I could feel my heartbeat speeding up as I spilled out a number of loaded questions. I immediately began to pray and summon God for help with my anxiety that was already evidenced by my sweaty hands and forehead.

I started speaking really fast to God and wondered if he was telling me to "Slow Down!" I just wanted to remind him that we had already buried one of our three sons and how traumatic and devastating it had been. I realized that it had been 33 years earlier, but it still feels like yesterday every time I think about our firstborn and how sweet, kind and caring this little four-year-old angel was. He had brought immeasurable joy into our lives and was probably the glue that held our shaky marriage together early on. He was a hugger and loved his mommy with all his heart!

I continued to remind God that it would be hard to survive another blow to our hearts and souls from the pain of losing another one of our children. As I continued packing our things so we could head back home…there was no doubt in my mind that God had not heard my numerous prayers. I would find out in a few hours that although he had heard them…some things still can only be explained as providence and divine order!

My main concern was just knowing that my 32-year-old baby boy was okay. Accidents happen all the time in our military town where everyone has gotten their driver's license from different states and countries, and everyone seems to make up their own driving rules. So maybe one of these under-skilled drivers had hit our son's vehicle and he was at the hospital being treated. My heart, my mind, my soul would not let me believe anything otherwise!

The four-hour drive home was heart-wrenching. I would later realize the photos I had glanced at on my phone of a tragic accident were actually photos of our son's accident!

After a long, tense ride home, we arrived. Finally, I sighed. *We made it.* Now all my questions would be answered and my nerves would settle down a little, or so I thought!

We parked and my husband told me to sit tight. At first, I told him that he must be out of his mind. I had no intentions of sitting still after waiting to go see DJ and make sure that he was okay! I finally agreed and my husband walked inside to get the details of what was going on.

He returned to the car after about five minutes and had a strange look on his face but said absolutely nothing. I took that as "Well, at least nothing tragic has happened."

This, I would find out, was far from the truth!

I opened the car door and started walking very slowly into our home and saw our surviving son. I knew by his concerned look that the news would not be good.

Post-traumatic triggers began to flood my emotions fairly quickly, as I recalled the familiarity of this scene. My mind began to race and go back to the time our first child died and I arrived at our in-laws'

ADULT TRAUMA: WHEN TRAUMA APPEARS TO BE CHASING YOU

home and saw so many cars there. I knew then that something serious had happened.

My son began to inform us about the details of Darius' accident, and I was really not listening to what he was saying. I just kept saying that we needed to get to the hospital immediately. It was when my sister came inside the house from our screened-in patio that I knew my prayers for God to not let another one of my children die had not been answered.

After our son shared that our sweet baby boy had died in the accident, I went into shock again. This time the impact from the trauma would hit even harder than before.

As my son tried his best to console me, the weight of my screams caused me to collapse in his arms as we both cried uncontrollably. I will never forget the words that my son spoke to me, "Mom, I need you. I need you, Mom! We will get through this together!" I ran into our bedroom and collapsed into my husband's arms as we relived what was a familiar scene it was from when our first child had died!

The first few hours after learning about the death of our second child, I found myself wanting to hide in our tiny closet. No place else seemed safe and no place else gave me the solace that I was longing for. I remember my sister coming in the room for the next few hours and finding me in the closet. I could tell that she was already worried about my mental and emotional state.

The hundreds of calls we received from all around the world was so comforting, but also overwhelming. So many people reached out to our family to see if they could help in any way. Some had begun to stop by our home, and after seeing a few close friends and breaking down uncontrollably with each visit, I could not take it any longer. I felt like running away from home for the first time in my life!

I told our sweet daughter-in-law to manage everything and to taper down the visits, calls and anything else so that our family could get some privacy and begin the painful task of planning our son's funeral, which we affectionately called his "Life Celebration!"

During the following weeks after we had buried our son, I could feel my body trying to collapse. I was starting to experience weird symptoms like my eyelids jumping uncontrollably and my throat burning and hurting like I had never experienced. This was such a difficult time to bury anyone because it was during the pandemic and Covid was rampant. Fortunately, none of us contracted Covid during this period or at least the home tests revealed that we had not.

The physiological symptoms I was experiencing I now know were evidence that trauma had hit my body and had dealt an unbelievable blow! One that would linger for years after things had returned to what we now know will never be "normal."

Most of the research has confirmed that the deepest grief, trauma and emotional wounding is from the death of a child. Yes, burying a spouse, a parent, a sibling, a cousin, aunt or uncle and best friend is traumatic as well, but I can clearly say after experiencing the deaths of two of our children, nothing comes even close in my sixty- plus years of living to the pain of burying your child.

As I previously mentioned, I have had to try and not be a compulsive worrier or overthinker when it came to my children's personal safety and well-being. I certainly had a good reason for feeling this way. Our son who was four years old had never been apart from me for not even a few hours and the very first time that I allowed him to go visit his grandparents without me, he was accidentally shot by a young boy cousin while they were playing hide-and-seek in my parents' bedroom closet.

I was a young twenty-five-year-old mother and my husband was just twenty-nine years old. We had only been married five short years and had dealt with quite a bit of relationship trauma and a ton of toxic encounters that had really taken a toll on both of us. As young parents,

ADULT TRAUMA: WHEN TRAUMA APPEARS TO BE CHASING YOU

we struggled with the fact that our marriage had taken a significant hit and one that would shape our marriage for years to come.

We both had grown up in families that had complicated family system dynamics, that included everything from parental alcohol addiction to physical and emotional abuse at extremely toxic levels. The death of our firstborn child, our sweet baby boy, Erran, would be the beginning of a trauma journey that we had no idea would last for years and years to come!

Absolutely nothing prepares a parent for the sudden and tragic death of their child. It is one of the most traumatic things that a parent might experience.

While all grief is significant and has its share of uncertainty, it is unnatural in the course of life to bury your children. My very faith was shaken to the core, and I grappled with the scripture about God having a good plan for our lives.

The scripture in Jeremiah 29:11 (Msg Bible) reads, "I know what I'm doing. I have it all planned out – plans to take care of you, not abandon you, plans to give you the future you hope for." Well, this certainly was not the future that I had hoped for, asked for or even imagined! Having to bury my little buddy before his fifth birthday and subsequently dealing with a life of trauma is why I felt that trauma had somehow chased me and at times, caught me and disrupted my life over and over again! When I think about how trauma has shaped my life, a part of me wonders how very different my life might have looked if so many traumatic things had not happened to me.

When I think about adult trauma, I think about all of the thousands of adults who have reported having been abused as a child, molested as a child, victims of domestic violence as a child, witnessed a parent being shot, or worse, killed as a child, who had an alcoholic parent who did or said terrible things to them as a child and all of the other horrible things that happen to children that are traumatizing and debilitating. This is why we are probably dealing with generations of trauma. It's time to confront the elephant in the room on a big level.

How could these things not affect a person as an adult, even with counseling and therapeutic intervention? This is exactly what *The Body Keeps the Score* is trying to tell us. Dr. Bessel Van Der Kolk has tried desperately to warn us about the permanent damage trauma can cause. He has tried to tell us that it is possible to feel safe again if we would confront and confess the reality of what has happened to us.

Even when we try and forget those childhood memories mentally, our bodies will not! This is because just as our cellular system has an imprint, so does our neurological system. Our bodies continue to store information on how trauma has affected us, and the evidence comes out in so many different ways. The impact of trauma is located in the "survival part" of the brain, which unfortunately, does not return to baseline after the threat is over.

Trauma affects the entire human organism—our thinking, feeling, behaviors, our relationships and the entire functioning of the human body. The very fact the PTSD (post-traumatic stress disorder) is one of the main issues with our military service members is evidence that long after the war is over and the military trainings have stopped, our bodies hold on to what happened to it and will only release after the proper processing or healing has taken place.

One powerful piece of evidence that was presented years ago that proved the power of childhood trauma and its effect was seen on an episode of The Oprah Winfrey Show. During the farewell season, two hundred men who had been molested came forward as part of a two-day event in 2010 to take a stand against sexual abuse. The show aired on November 5th, 2010.

The fact that these men had the courage to come forward after so many years had passed proves that they had not forgotten what had happened to them. The trauma was probably not very visible on the outside, but from their stories, the trauma was definitely still residing inside and had been there for quite some time.

If we could hear the personal stories from these men, they probably could attest to the fact that their childhood trauma had affected their lives in ways that were unimaginable. This is why it is so important for us to share our stories about trauma because it is the only way that things will change and people will begin to take courageous steps toward healing and wholeness.

I am writing this book to let others know that trauma must be confronted and not ignored or swept underneath the rug. Out of sight does not mean out of mind in this particular instance. Trauma is rampant currently in our country. Are we going to just sit idly by and do nothing? Or will we take a stand to ignite healing in our homes, in our land and in our bodies?

I further believe that a trauma-ridden society demands attention from policy makers and individuals who can really help things change. It is crucial for our government to begin to fund more programs and projects that help combat this all-important social issue.

It is my prayer that by sharing my very painful story and experiences with trauma others will realize the seriousness of managing our mental health and the importance of "working through our traumatic events" in order to have happy, healthy thriving lives and, more importantly, healthy marriages, relationships and thriving families! We must "Do the Work" if we really want to heal from trauma and its devastating impact!

Trauma indeed has chased me and it has chased so many others. At the final editing of this book, there are things that are happening in our country that are traumatizing for our nation. It was reported that in January 2025, California experienced the second most destructive fire in the state's history. More than 16,000 homes and other structures were damaged or destroyed.

Schools burned completely to the ground, which was devastating and traumatizing for teachers and children. Churches were lost, affecting pastors and parishioners alike. Family-owned businesses and companies that had been around for decades were wiped away in a matter of hours.

When trauma attacks in such a massive way, we must take our mental, emotional, psychological, economical and spiritual recovery and healing seriously. If not, the effects will show up years later and may not look anything like what we expect!

It is imperative that we run into paths of healing. These will help us to be productive, thriving citizens, employees, wives, husband, parents and friends. When we give fragments of ourselves to each other, it disables the concept of wholeness. It causes us to not be our authentic selves and only give portions of ourselves minute by minute. Eventually, we see the residue of this kind of coping mechanism, and it is not a pretty picture.

We must vow to stand up to *TRAUMA*. To not back down. When trauma continues to chase us, we must continue to run into paths of healing and wholeness so we can live out our healthy, happy lives and our vibrant legacies!

Questions for Reflection:

THOUGHTS:
Have you had a lot of traumatic experiences in your life? If so, how did you deal with them?

FEELINGS:

What are you feeling in your body after reading this chapter about how compounding trauma can affect us?

BEHAVIOR:

How have you healed from unrelenting trauma? What are some of the resources (paths) that you used that helped?

CHAPTER [4]
Relationship Trauma

In an earlier chapter of this book, I was trying to get people to understand that trauma does not look one particular way. There are so many faces of trauma, and they can look different on any given day. One common factor in all or most traumatic experiences is that it can last for decades.

Nowhere is this truer than in relationships. It could be in marriage, dating, working, business relationships, or platonic friendships. An individual's unhealed trauma can show up in any type of relationship and wreak havoc. By the time a couple might decide to seek help, for example, divorce may seem to be the only reasonable solution.

> A healthy relationship is one that should feel safe and supportive. Healthy relationships are built on trust, honesty, open communication and mutual respect. When these characteristics are missing, this should be of great concern to both people.

Relationships are the nucleus of everything in existence. We were created to connect, but how is that possible if unhealed trauma is preventing us from connecting with one another? So many times what we think is "relationship drama" turns out to be "trauma!" So many of us did not see healthy relationship modeling growing up and have been blindsided once we marry someone and then realize their childhood was riddled with trauma and, even worse, they have not healed from any of it!

Aside from the deaths of two of my children, some of my most painful and deepest trauma wounds have come from very close relationships. More specifically—my marriage! Some of it I have healed from and some of it is still requiring me to sit in the healing process a little longer.

One extremely important factor to remember when we marry our spouses is that we are marrying their past, their fears, their childhood traumas and triggers, their intergenerational trauma, their unhealed trauma, their mental health issues and the list goes on and on!

Most people are in search of healthy, happy relationships. I do not think anyone enjoys having a marriage or relationship that is full of toxicity and confusion. It is important to understand what a healthy relationship looks like in order to avoid the trauma that can come about if two people are not committed to safeguarding their relationship.

A healthy relationship is one that should feel safe and supportive. Healthy relationships are built on trust, honesty, open communication and mutual respect. When these characteristics are missing, this should be of great concern to both people.

The most important thing is to have standards and enforce them. Not knowing what to look for early on in a healthy, thriving relationship will lead to settling for much less.

It has taken me years to be able to talk about the abusive and serious nature of relationship trauma. Because of the sensitivity of this topic, I will not be using "real names" or sharing any deeply personal information. Whenever I write my books, I extend as much "grace" as possible because there is no blessing attached to getting healed at the expense of wounding someone else! However, it is my goal to share authentically so people's lives can be changed for the better. It is not my intention to further wound anyone who may already be dealing with unhealed trauma themselves.

However, because of the level of emotional and psychological trauma I have endured in the past forty-plus years of marriage, I do feel obligated to share and warn as many young ladies as possible about the dangers of marrying too young, getting involved with a "wolf" in sheep's clothing, being emotionally distracted and not staying focused on your life's goals, not understanding your personal worth and value, allowing low self-esteem to contribute to bad relationship decisions, trauma bonding and so much more!

So, let's dive into a conversation about relationship trauma!

Relationship trauma is the psychological, emotional, mental or physical harm caused by abuse and/or harm in an intimate or close relationship. It can be the result of betrayal, abandonment, infidelity, abuse, neglect and other subtle forms of emotional wounding.

Please understand that relationship trauma can have long-lasting effects on a person's mental, emotional and physical health. I have experienced this firsthand, and as I stated earlier, I feel extremely obligated to share my story in order to help others.

Some types of abuse from relationship trauma may look like:

- ❖ Emotional abuse
- ❖ Physical abuse
- ❖ Sexual abuse

- ❖ Belittling, insulting or bullying behavior
- ❖ Threatening behavior
- ❖ Controlling the victim
- ❖ Controlling or eliminating access to finances
- ❖ Intimidation (verbally or physically)
- ❖ Destruction of personal property
- ❖ Isolating the victim or some other type of entrapment
- ❖ Gaslighting (manipulating reality to make a partner question themselves)
- ❖ Love-bombing (attempting to influence a partner through insincere shows of love and affection)
- ❖ Stonewalling (not communicating with a partner/giving them the "silent treatment")
- ❖ Manipulation
- ❖ Power playing

While this is my story about how relationship trauma has affected me, I am certain everyone has their own story about relationship trauma and maybe even…relationship drama!

As a marriage and family therapy professional and a certified relationship coach, a lot of the relationship drama many of my clients are experiencing is not so much from "acting out" or being "extra." It is actually unhealed relationship trauma that is interfering with the health of their relationships. Once a distinction is made between conflicting emotional behavior and unhealed trauma wounds, then the process of effective intervention can begin.

RELATIONSHIP TRAUMA

I am writing this book in order to get people to see the importance of getting "healed" from trauma because even the impact of childhood trauma can manifest in so many ways, and many individuals who have experienced trauma may struggle with trust issues, intimacy, emotional regulation and even self-worth as an adult.

Unresolved emotional wounds can create a deep void within, which can lead to a yearning for a sense of belonging and emotional fulfillment. This inner void can make an individual susceptible to seeking validation and connection outside of their marriage or committed relationship. This is when infidelity comes into play. I will discuss later in this chapter how infidelity can be a profoundly traumatic event in and of itself!

Relationship trauma can be very complicated due to the vast number of extraneous variables that can affect what is happening. I am not a supporter of teen dating because the dynamics of a committed relationship can be overwhelming for a teen. They are still trying to figure so much out. Their lives are already full of decision-making! Adding a relationship to the equation causes problems. Plus, most teenagers are not equipped to handle the rejection that can come with a breakup and can become extremely sad or suicidal.

There have been a number of teen deaths related to fights over a boyfriend or girlfriend and murders due to issues related to breakups. As an adult, the pain and rejection from some of my relationship trauma was beyond overwhelming, so I can only imagine how a teenager or young adult who doesn't even have half of the coping/life skills that I have could possibly manage!

At the writing of this book, I have been married to my husband for forty-two (42) years! It's still hard for me to wrap my head around this fact. We met on a college campus when I was twenty-one and he was twenty-four years old. I had only had one boyfriend in high school for a short time prior to meeting my husband, so I really had not experienced any relationship trauma up to that point.

After meeting my husband, we both committed to seriously dating and considered each other to be off-limits to the dating pool. Or at least that was what I thought. From the very beginning, I saw red flags everywhere.

During the year we dated, I caught him cheating with other girls several times. There was even an incident where I had gone over to his apartment unexpectedly and he would not open the door. I stood there banging on the door for what seemed like hours (it was probably more like fifteen minutes) until he finally saw that I was not leaving and he opened the door!

This was very traumatizing emotionally because common sense told me he was hiding something. Normally when visiting his apartment, I was allowed to go anywhere I wanted, but during this visit, he demanded I not walk through the apartment. I decided to go to the bathroom, and he followed me to make sure I did not open his bedroom door.

Afterwards, I knew his morals and values were quite different than mine and that he had problems being loyal and committed. This pattern would continue for years, even into our marriage, and the amount of relationship/emotional trauma that has resulted is extremely hard to talk about. It's been staggering and unbelievable, if I can be perfectly honest.

Healing and repair in our marriage only came about through seeking God for direction and restoration and by going to marriage counseling, doing the inner work that is needed in order to heal and, most importantly, by being brutally open and honest with one another.

I cannot write about relationship trauma without addressing how infidelity can be a profoundly traumatic event and can lead to symptoms very similar to those seen in post-traumatic stress disorder

(PTSD). Some clinicians are actually starting to use the term "post-infidelity stress disorder" in an attempt to amplify the seriousness of this issue.

Infidelity causes some of the deepest trauma wounds of all relationship wounds! It cuts to the core question of "Am I good enough?" This causes a person to question their self-worth and the need to be validated often can make an already fragile situation break!

Infidelity was actually the culprit behind my first interaction with serious trauma. As a young military wife, there were so many things to adjust to and one of them was all the separations due to my husband being "deployed" or getting military orders for another duty station. This meant we were apart for months and sometimes years!

It is during this time that many spouses (both husband and wives) fall prey to infidelity. Unfortunately, the entire family unit suffers because someone decides to think only of themselves. The trauma from infidelity is far-reaching and has lasting effects on the entire family system!

Some may ask, "How is infidelity traumatic?" Infidelity involves a violation of trust, which is a fundamental aspect of every relationship. This violation can lead to feelings of betrayal, hurt and anger. When someone cheats on you, this can cause an entire range of emotions from extreme anger and anxiety to emotional distress and even rage!

It is crucial to recognize the trauma associated with infidelity and the need for healing and recovery. The betrayed partner needs time to process their emotions, to work through the emotional ups and downs and to work toward rebuilding trust, if they decide that they even want to.

The trauma of infidelity will affect the way you connect in the future with your spouse or significant other. In the therapeutic world, these connections are called "attachment styles." Attachment styles are blueprints for how people give and receive love. They are normally formed in childhood through interactions with parents and caregivers. They affect your adult romantic relationships and sometimes may need to be changed if the pattern is not serving you well. It's super important to have strong connections/attachments in order to have and keep your relationship healthy.

There are four main attachment styles:

- **Secure** – which is considered the healthiest. This style is characterized by trust, safety and a positive view of relationships. The majority of time, people with this style are comfortable with being alone and normally manage conflict very well.

- **Anxious** – people with this particular style have high anxiety issues and low avoidance. They may appear a little clingy and anxious about the possibility of abandonment.

- **Avoidant** – this style is characterized by emotional distance and many individuals are reluctant to depend on others. Although people with this style may appear independent, they still struggle with forming deep relationships.

- **Disorganized** – this attachment style is a mix of behaviors, often resulting from a significant amount of trauma or inconsistent caregiving.

RELATIONSHIP TRAUMA

Out of all the attachment styles, the relationship trauma from the early years in my marriage definitely caused me to have an "anxious attachment." This would last for years into our marriage. Just to summarize, an "anxious attachment style" is characterized by feeling insecure in a close relationship. This can mean that the individual desires 24/7 contact, which can be nerve-racking and very distracting.

A wife who has experienced several bouts of infidelity from her husband more than likely has this attachment style. She may find herself constantly texting her husband and anxiously awaiting a reply.

Therapy will be a "must" in order to heal from the trauma of infidelity. The goal should be to transition one day back into a "secure attachment style" because it is considered the healthiest form of attachment. Couples with this style are comfortable expressing their emotions in the relationship. They are comfortable with closeness and are not fearful about things going wrong as much. Even if the partner has to go out of town on a business trip or a military training, which was the case for me, the individual does not experience a sense of panic or fear.

This topic of relationship trauma is why I am so passionate about what I do. It is why I went back to graduate school when I was fifty-eight in order to become a marriage and family therapist. It is important for me to pour into other young ladies who are considering marriage or who are in committed relationships.

I really want young ladies to realize the high price they will pay emotionally if they ignore certain red flags. This is one time in life where ignorance can be extremely dangerous and can quite possibly cause permanent emotional scars/wounding.

Even after being armed with the best relationship information, no one is capable of changing another. That's up to the individual, and until there is an honest decision that will lead to change—nothing will happen! Change requires an honest decision, and many are not willing to do the work that is required.

Another note I would like to add here about relationship trauma is that certain traumatic events shake us to our core and may have a negative impact on our lives and even the foundation of self-development. I only wish I had realized the seriousness of not going to therapy in order to get support with my trauma wounds. I wish I had not waited so many years. One thing I know for sure, if we do not deal with our childhood trauma, our unresolved trauma issues and unresolved emotional wounds, they can and will impede the ability to form healthy, intimate thriving relationships in adulthood.

There is so much that I could say and write about in regards to relationship trauma at this point in my life. Some of it is still too painful to recount and even the Bible states that there are times when we should "move on" from the past.

> **13** No, dear brothers and sisters, I have not achieved it, but I focus on this one thing: Forgetting the past and looking forward to what lies ahead, **14** I press on to reach the end of the race and receive the heavenly prize for which God, through Christ Jesus, is calling us.
>
> —Philippians 3:13 (NLT)

The "forgetting" is the part that is difficult to do when significant unhealed trauma is still present. One of the most serious things that happens in many relationships that breaks the bond of trust and fidelity is infidelity. When a person decides to have an affair outside of the marriage or serious relationship, this is the beginning of a cycle of trauma that can cause permanent damage emotionally, mentally and even physically! Many relationships simply do not survive this trauma.

One of the most poignant stories I remember that signifies how trauma disrupts a relationship is the story about the female astronaut who drove cross-country more than fourteen hours and over 9,000 miles "in a diaper" (reportedly) to confront another woman about a man! What makes this story even more unbelievable is that the astronaut, Lisa Novak, was married and had three children, according to an article in the Denver Post.[1]

I remember hearing about this case when it happened back in 2007. I remember thinking, "What could possibly have happened to make this woman do this?" As I researched the event, I discovered there was some sort of "love triangle" going on. The more I learned, I understood how one woman became jealous of another woman's close relationship with a man that both women had deep feelings for.

This is something that we see quite often in relationships and most of it has a seed of trauma attached to it. Another reason that this story hits pretty close to home (and is fairly ironic) is that I had done something very similar to this early on in my marriage. I have my own version of driving over eighteen hours to confront my husband who was, at the time, an active duty serviceman in the military.

My husband had gone to a military school for training that lasted a few months. He had only been there two weeks when I called the barracks, which is where service members stay, only to be told that he had not been seen in a day or two! Well, I knew nothing had happened to him because I had been talking with him on the phone! But why was he not staying where he was supposed to be?

I was furious and had pretty much made up my mind that this repeated behavior was way too toxic for me to tolerate over and over again. The emotional trauma from experiencing this numerous times was taking a toll on my body, mind and soul!

My drive to the city where my husband was for training was just what I needed to really think about my future, my children's futures and if I wanted to stay married to someone in the military, which has its very own unique challenges to begin with. With every passing mile, I felt that I was looking back at all the years we had been together. As I drove, my mind began to wander and my thoughts bounced around as if they were a bouncy house of emotions. Just thinking about how many years were laced with emotional trauma from finding telephone numbers or suspecting some other emotionally charged thing might happen sent shockwaves throughout my body!

By the time I got there, I had calmed down quite a bit. Without going into every detail, I was furious when I first laid eyes on my husband, but after calming down (again!), we were able to talk about how we were going to get through yet another marital dilemma. Needless to say, we did move forward after months and maybe years of deciding to leave harmful and hurtful things in the past!

Before I talk about things that can cause trauma in a marriage or relationship, it's important to address the root of the problem. As I mentioned at the beginning of this chapter, we have no clue who we are really marrying. Even if you both grew up in the same hometown, it still doesn't mean that you are aware of another person's childhood traumas or emotional wounding.

I realized from our marriage that all of us have a certain amount of childhood trauma that can affect the dynamics of our relationships. It would be years before I understood that some of the marital issues surfacing in our marriage clearly had root causes of childhood trauma.

Sometimes, it may be easy to slip into an unhealthy relationship pattern because it's what some of us have seen modeled by our parents. If your parents did not have a safe, loving relationship, or were even divorced or living as roommates, this will more than likely affect your attachment style and how you handle relationship conflict. It's even possible that you have been through a series of toxic relationships yourself and may not have the awareness to recognize harmful patterns.

People who have experienced abuse in childhood often feel drawn to similar relationships in adulthood since the brain already recognizes the highs and the lows of the cycle. Many times, individuals have questioned how they continue to attract similar partners and also seem to be a human magnet for attracting toxic, unhealthy relationships.

The result of two people coming together who both have unhealed trauma and have had terrible examples of what a healthy marriage looks like normally end up in what is called a **"Trauma Bond."** A trauma bond is when a person forms a deep emotional attachment with someone that causes them harm, either emotionally or physically.[2] Trauma bonds can form as a result of an abusive cycle. It is important to note that abuse is not always physical; emotional abuse is abuse, too.

Trauma bonds are an unhealthy form of emotional attachment and can significantly impact your relationship. Trauma bonds, more times than not, are rooted in some form of abuse. Abusive relationships can be tricky, because they normally start off like a fairy tale! Before the cycle of abuse starts, there is an initial honeymoon phase. The abuser will more than likely practice love bombing (showering their partner with gifts, affection, attention and over-the-top acts of service).[3]

Leaving an abusive relationship is especially difficult for young women who are unsure where they are going to live and how they are going to take care of their children. This is why so many women remain in unhealthy, unsafe relationships for so long and, in some cases sadly enough, some of them lose their lives due to not having another way out of the abusive situation.

It is my life's mission now to mentor, coach and advocate for young women who are smart, intelligent and hard-working, but who have landed in a situation where she feels "stuck" or feels that she has made one of the worst decisions of her life. Even if the decision is made to leave the relationship, there may still be difficulty in breaking the bond without seeking professional help. I have seen so many young women eventually return to abusive or toxic situations just because they feel "incomplete" or lost without their significant other. They choose the abusive cycle because it is familiar and feels "safe." However, once they get stronger emotionally, they realize that they can do much better alone and finally leave for good!

Unfortunately, I can relate to this because I married way too young (when I was twenty-one) and realized just a few months into my marriage that my young husband of twenty-four was not equipped and had carried most, if not all, of his unhealthy relationship habits into our marriage. He really thought he could be married and single at the same time. Needless to say, this caused us to have tons of problems in the early years of our marriage.

I realized that I had ignored every single "red flag" during our year of dating and that some of the behavior I saw was a direct result of his unhealed trauma from childhood! So much of the toxicity in our marriage and relationships manifests early on, but most of the time we are either naïve or just in denial about what we are seeing. I am convinced that the high rate of divorce is because many have swept their trauma underneath the rug instead of going to counseling or therapy to deal with the toxic behavior that is destroying the marriage.

RELATIONSHIP TRAUMA

> Building healthy relationships take work—big work! There is no such thing as "cutting corners" in a great marriage or relationship.

Most people have no idea that "trauma bonding" is the problem in their marriage and that if this gets fixed…the marriage could thrive. It's only natural to desire to bond and connect with the person that you love, especially if they treat you with kindness the majority of time. Many individuals remember the early and happier days of their relationship and really believe the person will go back to who they were then. They realize all too late this is somewhat of a fantasy!

It is my prayer that by reading this book, many young women will see my how my resilience, courage and determination played an important role in my not giving up in marriage, in my career and in my life! I encourage young men and women to heal from any childhood trauma or other emotional trauma prior to getting married.

Building healthy relationships take work—big work! There is no such thing as "cutting corners" in a great marriage or relationship. There has to be some form of daily relationship maintenance and a commitment to fix issues fairly quickly because the longer the problems go unchecked…the greater the opportunity for a small flame to turn into a huge forest fire!

Questions for Reflection:

THOUGHTS:

After reading this chapter, would you say you have experienced some form of relationship trauma?

FEELINGS:

What are you feeling in your body after reading this chapter about how relationship trauma can shape our lives?

BEHAVIOR:

What, if anything, will you change about your life after reading this chapter?

CHAPTER [5]
Socioeconomic & Financial/Poverty Trauma

Being raised in poverty can have devastating effects on a child and can be the first interaction with trauma that is lasting. A child going to bed hungry because there is no food in the house and not able to go to sleep as a result—is beyond sad. This same child who gets up in the morning to attend school and has no breakfast is now put in a position where he or she is not alert, possibly irritable and cognitively challenged. This is possibly how many children get "left behind!"

The teacher has no idea what the child is dealing with but screams at the child or disciplines them unknowingly for something that is out of their control! This type of trauma never leaves the brain or the body and is probably one of the reasons workaholic adults exist.

Most of these adults vow to never be hungry again or never live without lights or warm water, so they work nonstop in order to secure their financial futures. All while ignoring the fact that their childhood trauma is the culprit. Trauma could create a "cycle" of poverty!

Poverty trauma is behind so many behavior patterns and some of them, while not necessarily bad, are not healthy either! Financial challenges and hardships can be a source of trauma, and we are seeing this more and more in our society. Financial struggles bring about a lot of stress and unwanted traumatic experiences. There are individuals who live in a constant fear of never having enough and some of them have been diagnosed with "hoarding disorder."

Socioeconomic trauma is a type of emotional pain that results from poverty and lack of financial support. It adds layers of emotional stress and affects marriages and the entire dynamics of the family system. Studies have shown that people with low socioeconomic status have higher rates of trauma, which should not be surprising because not having your basic needs met is not only distracting but can leave a lifelong imprint on a person's brain and childhood memory bank.

I believe that socioeconomic trauma directly affects pregnant mothers who experience food scarcity thus contributing to lower birth weight or smaller babies, along with a host of other deficiencies. Trauma can and does manifest as early as infancy as failure to thrive, growth delays, sleep disruption and many other developmental issues.

Not addressing trauma that is the result of socioeconomic disparities can be extremely costly to organizations as well. Unhealed trauma can be linked to chronic illnesses, physical accidents, interpersonal violence, emotional abuse, financial hardships, high job absenteeism and so much more, all directly affecting the bottom line and cost to run a company. The economic and social costs to families, communities, companies/organizations and to society comes to hundreds of billions of dollars each year.

Trauma is a problem that touches almost every area of our lives, including financially, and is definitely one that should not be ignored.

Growing up in a family of nine (seven children plus two adults) meant that our grocery bill was a weekly conversation piece. My parents did a great job making sure that we did not go to bed hungry, however, now that I am older, I understand how Blacks/African Americans are the dominant race with high-blood pressure are, diabetes, heart disease and a few other health issues. As a child, I remember eating a huge amount of pork and tons of red meat almost on a daily basis.

One of my favorite meals as a child of eight or nine years of age was "fried pork chop." I remember it as if it were yesterday, asking my mother for TWO pieces of pork chops, when we barely had enough to go around for the nine of us! LOL. Talk about food scarcity. I remember running out of milk for cereal and my older siblings mixing canned milk with water in order to still enjoy their favorite food.

Our family was not the only family in this poor community who had to constantly try and make ends meet. As I think back, most of the families had a large number of children in them and were probably having to supplement food shortages as well. Many who are reading this book may not be able to relate to this type of trauma, but that still doesn't mean that it did not exist or that it is irrelevant.

Writing this book has been a huge wake-up call for me now that I am in my early sixties. My heart goes out to all the children who are going to sleep at night and to school in the morning with empty stomachs. I now believe that we should have mandated programs where children can get breakfast prior to starting school and that checks and balances are performed to ensure a child is not hungry prior to instruction starting.

Now, I am aware that some schools have breakfast programs, but many of the children get to school late, some will choose not to get the food for whatever reason and some may not even be aware that the food is available. It does not matter if breakfast has to be incorporated into the instruction time…going without food is a form of trauma that is preventable, and we must make sure that more is being done!

Not only was food scarcity a form of trauma in my childhood, but there were also other forms of financial trauma present too. I remember when I was in the third or fourth grade going to school with dirty sneakers on and seeing another classmate with brand new white sneakers. It made me sad enough to cry. Not because mine were dirty, but because I knew it would be a while before my parents could buy me some new ones. I knew this because I overheard my dad talking about how high the electrical bill was and how he had to work overtime in order to keep the lights on.

Kids who grew up in wealthy families cannot even begin to fathom this type of humiliation, and many of them will never know this face of trauma. Again, it is amazing how trauma shows up in ways we least expect from childhood to adulthood and beyond. Healing from childhood trauma is a process that could take a lifetime depending on how much a person was affected.

There was other evidence of financial trauma and socioeconomic disparities in our small poor community. We had a long railroad track that literally separated the black community from the white community. While the black community had a few brick homes or a few nice homes with siding, it appeared that the white community had the nicer brick homes and nicer business establishments, most of which had been owned by white families for generations.

Ironically, the schools, grocery stores, fast food restaurants, laundromats, gas stations, department stores and library was located closer to the white community. This always puzzled me, but I never thought about it long enough for it to affect me. Now that I am old enough to analyze it all, it was subtleties like this that was the seed of financial trauma and lack that could have scarred me for life, but I thank my heavenly Father it did not!

Fast forward to 1982, the first year of our marriage. We decided to elope, so I flew from North Carolina to Colorado Springs, Colorado, to become Mrs. Dawson. Neither of us had a clue what we were signing up for at such a young age (we were in our early twenties). I now understand why people have weddings, receptions and gift registries because although we had an apartment, there was absolutely nothing in it! No pots, pans, towels, rugs, sheets or even food! This would be our first lesson in financial trauma, but it would by no means be our last!

I understand why the divorce rate is so high in the first few years of marriage. It's because most of the conflict and division probably steams from financial problems (money)! This is actually what most studies have shown. This is what I call "preventable trauma." We can prevent the emotional scars and trauma that comes along with financial disasters if we would make better choices. Unfortunately, love can be blinding, and most young people feel that they have all the answers only to look back to see how most of the financial trauma early on was self-inflicted!

There is so much I could say about the financial trauma I experienced during the early years of our marriage, but that will have to be in another book at another time!

Although most of my financial trauma occurred during the early years of our marriage, it would take years for me not to be affected by the fear of "not having enough." There was the fear of running out of money each month and the fear that something might be turned off due to a bill not getting paid…Financial fear is hard to forget when it occupies so much of your life and brain space!

I remember around year eight in our marriage going outside to go to work and take our sons to daycare and our car was…gone! To make matters worse, this was during a time when my husband and I had gone through a short separation while we both tried to manage the grief and emotional pain from losing our four-year-old son. Things had gone from bad to worse quickly and I felt that my entire world was falling apart. In some ways, it was!

So, after opening the door and discovering that the only mode of transportation I had was missing, I totally "crashed out" as the young people say now. I did not scream or make a scene because I did not want to startle my boys, but I was a wreck. For some reason, my mind would not let me entertain a scenario of the car being stolen. All I remember is that I was two payments behind. I thought I had one more month before the company would show up to recover. Boy was I absolutely wrong!

I was able to call a few family friends to help me get the total amount that was due (and the additional fees for repossession), but to this day I vividly remember how it felt to open the door and not see my vehicle out there. To say that it was traumatic is an understatement!

I do not believe I am the only person who has experienced this type of financial trauma. The bottom line is that financial trauma is trauma, and it confirms the fact that "trauma looks different" at any given time.

I am praying that some young couple will read this book and decide to live within their means no matter what so they will not experience unnecessary financial trauma. Only take vacations when it will not put you further behind financially once you return home. We never lived above our means…our problem was never that, we just never had enough to make ends meet until years later in our marriage.

Now one thing that I would like to share is how we coped with the stress from experiencing financial trauma continuously for so many years. As I think back on all the times we were short on money and

SOCIOECONOMIC & FINANCIAL/POVERTY TRAUMA

had to rob Peter to pay Paul, Silas, and Timothy—it was not a good feeling at all. I remember how my body shook when my vehicle was repossessed and how my chest felt when I didn't have enough money to cover the daycare bill. And I remember the three-day-long headache that came after I was embarrassed at the grocery store counter when my card was declined. Not to mention leaving behind my entire cart I had taken over an hour to fill!

I am realizing while writing this book that I never shared this in therapy—not even once. I have suppressed these memories in the same manner that many of you are suppressing your trauma and hoping it will never rear its ugly head, but chances are…the minute you are standing at the cash register and realize you left your wallet at home…the trauma triggers will remind you of the time some twenty years before because…the body keeps the score!

One of the most devastating accounts of financial trauma came in January 2010. Both of our sons had graduated from college. We were so proud of them both because they had done exceptionally well in college and did not give us any problems whatsoever. Prior to them going to college, we vowed we would sacrifice for them to have cars and not have to rely on others for rides.

As parents, we realized being a "rider" took away some of our sons' control. If the driver had been drinking alcohol or under the influence of some other substance, our sons' lives could be in danger, and we were not willing to take that chance. So, making sure they had their own vehicles was a financial hardship we were willing to accept.

Our middle son had expressed that he really wanted a certain car for his graduation gift: an almost new black special edition Chevrolet Impala. It was not really within our budget, but he had made us so proud by graduating with "honors" as a student-athlete. I remember the day we surprised him with it on campus. He was a wide receiver (and a star player) on the football team, and they were just finishing up practice. We wanted to give it to him while the team was still outside, and when our son realized we were dropping off his car, well—I've never seen his eyes that big. He even looked a little teary-eyed. Little did we know he would only be able to enjoy his special gift for eighteen months, if that.

At any rate about eighteen months later, I remember him calling us early one morning. Both had graduated from college and had moved to Atlanta. They were roommates and they both had jobs. His voice sounded like he had been running. "My car is gone!" he said. I asked, "What do you mean…gone?" He said it was not in the parking deck. I asked if this was a joke. He assured me he would do no such thing. He had looked through the entire apartment complex prior to calling us and could not locate it. We all begin to panic as we realized that we had not put a tracking device on the vehicle yet.

After calling the police, our auto insurance and finance companies, we discovered the vehicle was in fact stolen. We were shocked. I could not stop crying. I knew exactly how much we had sacrificed financially to buy our son that car. We knew then that we had made an "emotional" financial decision, one that we really could not afford.

The financial trauma that ensued was beyond belief. Not only did we have a balance on the auto loan, but our son was now without a car, and we had no idea when we would be able to buy another one. The Georgia State Bureau of Investigation and local police determined there was a high-tech car theft ring in Atlanta and that several vehicles had been stolen. They shared that the thieves more than likely took the stolen cars to body shops where they were immediately painted, serial numbers taken off and either resold or shipped out of the country!

We never recovered our son's car and, to this day, the financial trauma from that incident still affects me. I have accepted the fact that attachment to material items should be distanced, because we cannot take them with us whenever we leave this world! So, when the disturbing thoughts about this incident flood my emotions, I immediately block them by thinking about more pleasant things. I am well aware this is a trigger that could bring about some unwanted trauma responses, so I adjust fairly quickly.

This is only one example of financial trauma, but there are probably a number of people who can share their own version of how financial trauma has affected them. Socioeconomic and financial trauma can affect us in similar ways, and we must understand that and be willing to seek intervention for it as we do other types of traumas.

Questions for Reflection:

THOUGHTS:

After reading this chapter, would you say you have experienced any financial, poverty or socioeconomic trauma in your life?

FEELINGS:

What are you feeling in your body after reading this chapter about how financial trauma can shape our lives?

BEHAVIOR:

What, if anything, will you change about your life after reading this chapter?

CHAPTER [6]
Understanding Intergenerational Trauma

Trauma has a memory bank filled with memories we would rather forget. When parents do not heal from their inner emotional wounds and trauma, there is a high likelihood that it will be repeated by other generations in the family. Generational trauma gets passed down through generations until someone has the courage to "break the toxic cycle" and decide that total healing is the pathway that must be taken!

As a member of the Black/African American race, I can attest to there being generations of trauma and emotional wounding, even as far back as "Slavery." The violence, oppression, discrimination and racism towards African Americans for generations have had lasting impacts on black families and communities.[1] Research shows that descendants of enslaved people experience higher rates of fear, hopelessness, anger, anxiety, mental health issues, addiction and more.

Intergenerational or **"transgenerational/generational trauma"** is the subconscious passing of traumatic experiences to future generations. Sometimes referred to as family trauma because it affects the entire family system and community, this type of trauma can manifest in so many ways, to include mentally, emotionally, socially or biologically. It can also be seen as **"collective trauma"** when it affects many individuals within a group. This is definitely seen in poor communities and economically deprived families where education and awareness are not as prevalent.

As a young girl, whenever we would study the history of slavery in school, I could feel my anxiety heighten. We learned about how wives watched their husbands being dragged off and sold to another slave owner or how wives were raped by their owners and the children sold and moved to different plantations. It was beyond traumatic to hear about it, so I can only imagine how it affected the families who experienced it! What we now know as intergenerational trauma is not only a "soul wound"—it is a lifelong scar that when touched, still yields pain from that which our ancestors had to endure.

It is especially time for the black race to heal from generations of wounding, to ultimately shed the trauma responses that our families and communities have experienced and begin to replace these trauma responses with healthy, thriving and adaptive coping strategies. When trauma has been passed down, it can manifest as so many other symptoms and diseases, such as diabetes, high blood pressure, heart disease, kidney disease, cancer, autoimmune disorders, depression and more that are seen solely or at least are more prevalent in the black community.

More and more research is revealing that stress-related chronic disease can and does run through generations of families. Exposure to toxicity as a result of adverse childhood experiences (ACEs) has been associated with chronic inflammation and so many diseases in general. Heart disease and a myriad of other chronic illnesses that persist into adulthood have been linked to psychological abuse suffered early on.

UNDERSTANDING INTERGENERATIONAL TRAUMA

> When trauma has been passed down, it can manifest as so many other symptoms and diseases, such as diabetes, high blood pressure, heart disease, kidney disease, cancer, autoimmune disorders, depression and more that are seen solely or at least are more prevalent in the black community.

Pain and trauma have a way of traveling throughout generations and can show up in toxic relationships. It can be disguised as self-sabotaging behavior, toxicity of some form, alcoholism, drug abuse, sexual abuse or other addictive behaviors. All of these unhealthy coping mechanisms tend to be the demise of black families for generations until someone is brave enough to say, "Enough!"

Even if we did not play a part in creating the intergenerational trauma that exists, it is our moral/cultural duty and responsibility to "heal" from it and, more importantly, thrive in it! Our children deserve to live in communities that are thriving and that look healed and whole, instead of drug invested, emotionally, mentally and economically enslaved communities that are far from thriving but simply surviving.

Why is this phenomenon of intergenerational trauma now being talked about so much? One reason is that individuals whose parents or grandparents and maybe even great-grandparents experienced trauma are now experiencing some of the fallout from it. We are now learning more about how trauma can be passed down culturally. Unhealthy behaviors from parents or other family members can be modeled and thereby passed down to children and grandchildren.

Research is now showing that DNA can "remember" traumatic experiences and then pass down the effects of those experiences to multiple generations. As I have mentioned in the beginning of this book, our bodies have genetic codes and the brain and nervous system have ways to hold on to information much like a computer hard drive.

In the book *Break the Cycle*, Dr. Mariel Buque shares extensively about intergenerational trauma. She does an excellent job of explaining the dynamics of this type of trauma and shares that "unlike physical wounds, emotional wounds can reach beyond the person who is hurt and have the capacity to hurt others, like family members, significant others, friends, coworkers and children." She further elaborates that for this reason, unhealed emotional wounds can have devastating effects on entire families and communities.

Intergenerational trauma can have significant impacts on the family and on an individual's health and well-being. It can increase the risk of developing mental health disorders, chronic diseases and even have an impact on social problems in the community. Intergenerational trauma can lead to cycles of poverty, violence and addiction. We see this a lot in the inner city and in communities where poverty continues to repeat.

Now that we are able to understand what intergenerational trauma is, let's look at the ways it can be transmitted across multiple generations within a family or community.

One way is through **direct exposure.** This is when children witness or experience traumatic events themselves and then develop symptoms of trauma. Parental modeling is another mode of transmission. This is simply when parents have experienced trauma and then model unhealthy coping mechanisms or behaviors in front of their children. **Epigenetics** is when trauma can alter gene expression or genetic codes and then this gets passed down to offspring. To summarize, it's when trauma can be passed down through genetic changes to a person's DNA after they experience a significant amount of trauma.

So, as we can see, intergenerational trauma is very complex and can be a challenging issue that can have far-reaching consequences. It is more important now than ever before that we begin to understand the mechanisms of transmission, symptoms and potential for healing for individuals and communities alike. We must take this type of trauma seriously as well and begin to heal our families and communities. We can break the cycles and begin to promote well-being for future generations. Although this subject of intergenerational trauma is really of great concern currently, every family experiences generational trauma.

It is important to note that generational trauma patterns or cycles of trauma are unhealthy behaviors and relationships styles that are passed down through families when trauma isn't properly healed. We tend to see a lot of generational trauma in families where violence, abuse, alcoholism or drug use is paramount. The emotional impact can affect future generations, even if they did not directly experience the first traumatic event themselves.

Sometimes, it is difficult to break a cycle of generational trauma because much of the trauma is deep-rooted and widespread. It can be difficult for healing to begin when everyone is using the same unhealthy way of communicating and processing their emotions. It is especially difficult for the young members of the traumatized family or community to learn a better way of dealing with their trauma. The best thing for them to do is to get some external help/support.

CHASED BY TRAUMA

Upon writing this book, the subject of generational/family trauma began to really intrigue me. I began to think about my family of origin and wondered how generational trauma might be responsible for some of my relationship patterns. I thought about the times when I was a young girl and I saw my parents get into physical altercations and how that affected me. I was terribly frightened every time it happened, and when I would think about it years later (even into adulthood), I could feel anxiety and tension rise in my body. It also made me wonder if some of my early years of anger issues were connected to these events.

There are probably individuals who experienced similar situations and can probably relate to these feeling as well. Then there are cases of close friends and extended family who were raised in environments where alcoholic parents would be full of rage and anger when they were intoxicated and then be calm after they returned to themselves. These mental imprints can certainly cause generational trauma to be present. It amazes me how trauma touches our lives in countless ways, and it further confirms why this topic is one that should not be ignored or suppressed but one that should be taken very seriously.

I understand now how generations of alcoholics are in a family and how some children tend to repeat their parents' toxic habits, some without even knowing that they are victims of intergenerational trauma. As it pertains to the black race (which is the only one that I really know about and the one that I identify with culturally), I wonder whether some of our generational trauma isn't self-inflicted. Are we being too forgiving and allow our family members to continuously hurt or abuse us emotionally, just to "keep" the peace?

It made me wonder if we are programmed to respond to disrespect, disloyalty, betrayal and so much more—with understanding because we are "Blood!" We allow our loved ones to scar us with their harsh or hurtful words, their meanness and evildoings. This is not healthy and probably explains how generational/family trauma has gone on for so many years.

The psychological side of this type of trauma stems from how toxic family relationships contribute to us compromising who we really are just to stay in relationship with a family member who is not good for us. It encourages "codependency" and unhealthy attachment styles.

Here are a few common generational trauma patterns:

- Unhealthy coping – This can show up in a variety of behaviors such as aggression, anger, substance abuse or withdrawing from others to manage stress or pain.
- Trust and relationship issues – Unresolved trauma may prevent people from connecting with their family and loved ones.
- Avoiding talking about emotions – Family members may avoid talking about their feelings or the trauma, which will lead to emotional suppression. When we continue to allow others into our emotional space without addressing conflict concerns, this causes the generational trauma to continue.

While intergenerational trauma is a very complex and will require a commitment from the entire family if healing is to be taken seriously, Dr. Mariel Buque reminds us in her book Break the Cycle that healing future generations is possible.

> While nothing can be done about the past generational trauma, we can start right where we are and show our children positive ways to handle conflict, anxiety, anger and so much more.

She encourages all of us to be the change that we are needing. She challenges all of us to ask the question, "How do I wish to impact my future generations?" She suggests ways that we can begin to impact future generations by:

- Teaching them about nervous system regulation as a natural way to care for themselves, so that they do not experience some of the same suffering as their ancestors
- Creating a relationship with them that is rooted in safety and connection, so that they see you as a safe haven
- Engaging in advocacy that can help create safe environments
- Modeling behavior that you know will help them build a healthy self-esteem and a healthy self-concept
- Investing time in disrupting systems that dull their light and leave room for trauma to take root
- Finding ways to build resilience and stay hopeful

Learning so much about intergenerational trauma has really been an eye-opener for me. It brought about awareness to this very serious family issue. I still believe the number one way to begin to reframe what has happened is by modeling great behavior as parents and role models.

While nothing can be done about the past generational trauma, we can start right where we are and show our children positive ways to handle conflict, anxiety, anger and so much more. Trauma affects the soul, spirit and mind and requires profound healing. Healing will not and cannot happen overnight. There is a process to healing and no shortcuts are available.

It is so important to get support by going to therapy or finding a trusted counselor who specializes in emotional wound healing who will come alongside you and walk through a path of healing designed only for you. Sometimes because of a long history of emotional pain, suffering and psychological trauma, anxiety often tricks people into believing that their worries are endless. This is when trusting God to see you through the entire healing process is crucial.

Questions for Reflection:

THOUGHTS:

After reading this chapter, do you think you have inherited any generational trauma?

FEELINGS:

What are you feeling in your body after reading this chapter about intergenerational trauma?

BEHAVIOR:

What, if anything, might you change about your life after reading this chapter?

CHAPTER [7]
Spiritual Trauma a/k/a "Church Hurt"
When the Blessing...Breaks Us!

It is impossible to write about trauma and leave out the impact that spiritual wounds have on people. Unfortunately, people do not like to talk about the trauma or emotional scars from being spiritually traumatized. There really is a plethora of unaddressed soul wounds and emotional injury that have not been addressed. It has been going on for decades (especially in the black church). From my point of view, only temporary solutions were "slapped" over a much larger and more serious dilemma.

So yes, there are casualties in the church. Most of the wounds cannot be seen, but they are still there. Trauma doesn't discriminate—even in church settings. So, what happens when the very place we look to for support to heal disappoints us or—even worse—abandons us!? What happens when we dare to believe in God for healing from our trauma and turn to the church only to be "let down" or wounded even more? How can we possibly feel *safe* when the blessing...breaks us?

In moments of distress, everyone has their own way of coping and searching for various paths of healing. Many people tend to turn towards coping mechanisms that make it easier for them with their trauma. For many, it might be support groups or therapy but for so many, the church is where they turn for trauma care and encouragement. People are seeking solace and strength in God's word in order to endure their life struggles and trauma. This is the last place most people would think more layers of hurt would be added!

This spiritual trauma is often called **"church hurt"** or **"church trauma"** and it is a term used to describe the emotional and spiritual harm that individuals are experiencing as a result of their interactions within the church setting.

By the way, church hurt is not some made up term that individuals are using just to get attention. Church hurt is *REAL*, and it causes real pain. We may all have contributed to it either knowingly or unknowingly at some point because we all are humans and humans are subject to fall.

This chapter is very near and dear to my heart because I know as a professional mental health counselor/coach that the number one rule of therapeutic engagement is to "Do No Harm!" This should be even more true in the church of all places!

Even before I had accepted Christ into my life when I was thirteen, I had been in church my entire life. I played the piano for the youth choir, and I came from a strong lineage of bold Christians who believed that God could do anything!

I had often heard growing up the church being likened to a "hospital" where the wounded could come to be healed. But how can a church be a "spiritual hospital" for the deeply wounded, emotionally crippled and the beyond hopeless to come and be consoled and ministered to if people can be exploited anywhere? As much as we

SPIRITUAL TRAUMA A/K/A "CHURCH HURT"

want to believe that everyone on this Earth is "good," this is farthest from the truth. Evil is always close by when good is present.

But did I still believe God could do anything after the tragic death of our second child? My faith had been shaken. From my point of view, it appeared God had left me alone to figure it all out by myself. Where was God, and why was I still hurting so bad and feeling so lonely and abandoned? My faith had pulled me out of some very dark and painful places before, but I was still doubtful that a simple prayer would just zap this deep, deep emotional pain away in a matter of seconds!

I wanted to believe that I could go to the church for comfort, and I had done just that after the tragic death of our first child. However, some of the same people who I wanted to reach out to for support were people who had emotionally wounded me and never even came back to apologize!

It's probably hard to wrap your head around someone being traumatized in the church, but this is an age-old problem. It is time that everyone realizes that if someone is hurting, regardless of if they are at church, home, work, the grocery store or anyplace—they need to be heard. It someone has been neglected, abused or mistreated, it needs to be appropriately handled.

There are various forms of hurt and abuse that can be found in the church. Specific cases exist and several reported incidents/allegations of child sexual abuse in the Catholic church and other religious-based organizations, such as the Boys Scouts, have surfaced for years.

According to an NBC News article dated July 1, 2021, the Boys Scouts reached a $850 million settlement with tens of thousands of sexual abuse victims. The settlement was reportedly "the largest in a child sexual abuse case in United States history." This is just a fraction of the abuse, hurt and emotional pain that has happened in the church.

It would take months and years for me to accept that the only way total healing would even be possible was by surrendering the deep pain and suffering I was experiencing to God. The load was way too heavy for me to carry. The longer I denied this fact, the more my future seemed to fade from view.

I longed for answers as to why God would allow one family to experience so much tragedy and trauma. One scripture that helped me to start surrendering my pain to God was Psalm 27:8 where God is saying, "I have heard your cries for help, but you must come to me if you desire healing." I was still reluctant to ask for help because I had asked for help before and did not get what I was looking for, or at least…did not think I had!

I would soon discover that total healing from not just trauma but from anything is utterly impossible outside of God! Yes, there are lots of quick remedies and self-made solutions that will make us feel better temporarily. When it comes to trauma, quick fixes are a waste of time because a "bandage" will only work for so long. This is all the more reason why the church should be the place that many can turn to for solutions to heal. That's why spiritual trauma/church hurt is probably the worst kind of trauma to be dealing with.

> Psalm 27:8 (NLT) My heart has heard you say, "Come and talk with me." And my heart responds, "Lord, I am coming."

One thing I have continued to see is how so many people turn to the wrong things to try and soothe their triggers and heal their trauma wounds. By the time they finally admit that nothing is working, things have gone from bad to worse or to the point of no return. I often suggest to wounded people who are needing help to not wait until the house has "totally burned down" to call 9-1-1!

Sometimes it is difficult for people to put their trust in God when they are hurting so deeply. I was no exception. Even though I had been saved (a Believer) since my childhood, the trauma from losing two of my children really tested my faith at levels that I did not think was possible. People who have not buried one of their children or grandchildren can still praise God at levels that they are used to, but what happens when God starts taking things away from you or allows things to be taken? Can you still praise Him? Can you still worship and serve at the high levels that you were doing prior to the trauma?

Wrestling with my emotions caused me to question if I wanted to turn to God for my healing. Or, did I want to try and find answers myself? I have come to realize that while finding the answers ourselves is still an option, what we do not consider is that some answers have to be discovered; they are there, but hiding in plain sight! We risk going through even more pain and trauma when we try and do things outside of God. I and so many others have realized this because we did not create ourselves. The one who created us knows exactly what we need and what will make us operate at our very best—our most optimum levels! It's baffling though when we do not trust God for the answers when He knows our life story better than we do and why wouldn't He—He wrote it!

> People who have not buried their children or grandchildren can still praise God at levels that they are used to, but what happens when God starts taking things away from you? Can you still worship and serve at the high levels that you were doing prior to the trauma?

Now that we have talked about what qualifies as spiritual trauma aka "church hurt," we can quantify what church hurt is not! Church hurt is not a normal disagreement when someone sees things differently and respectfully communicates that. Just because your feelings got hurt does not justify you leaving the church!

"Church hurt" or spiritual trauma should also not be confused with "accountability," when someone asks us to explain ourselves or ask some tough questions about our lifestyle or something else that is not in alignment with us being a Christ follower.

It's extremely important to examine if the experience fits within the parameters of what church hurt is or is not. The Bible encourages us all to get along to the best of our ability. Romans 12:18 states, "If it is possible, as far as it depends on you, live at peace with everyone." This scripture should be on our hearts when we are tempted to approach someone about something that may be controversial.

Ironically, the history of "church/spiritual trauma" dates back to biblical days. There is a passage in the Bible, John 8:3-11 that literally addresses how to deal with church hurt. In this passage, the scribes and Pharisees bring a woman caught in adultery to Jesus, seeking his judgment, but Jesus, instead of condemning the woman, tells them that any one of them who are "without sin" should cast the first stone, prompting the accusers to each leave, one by one. When all of them had finally left, Jesus tells the woman to "go and sin no more."

SPIRITUAL TRAUMA A/K/A "CHURCH HURT"

What happened in this passage is also happening in the modern-day church in various forms. Women are being disciplined, but many times the men are not ostracized or even identified!

I am familiar with cases myself where a young girl gets pregnant (sometimes by the pastor's son or a close relative) but the girl is asked to immediately "go to the back and stay out of sight" until things are back to normal, if there is such a thing as "getting back to normal" after an event such as this!

While writing this book about church trauma, I came across a case where this young lady got pregnant and had been serving in one of the ministries in the church. One Sunday morning, the pastor made a public announcement that the young girl would no longer be allowed to function in her role in the church and was further instructed to sit on the back pews until instructed otherwise. Talk about emotional trauma, scarring and shaming—this was terrible!

I also experienced church hurt and trauma in a particular church. This was within the last few years, and it hurt so deeply that I slipped into a short depression. My situation was a result of requesting a meeting with the senior pastor and his wife due to some serious issues I was having with an in-law overstepping her boundaries as it pertained to our marriage. Had my husband taken responsibility for allowing the behavior, the meeting might not have been necessary. He did not though, and this forced me to take the lead and get help because it was affecting our marriage in a big way.

So, all parties involved were in this meeting and I preceded to share how I felt "defenseless" as a wife due to my husband allowing one of his sisters to occupy way too much of his time. This was happening during a time when our marriage was not in the best shape, mainly because both of us were still grieving the tragic death of our second child. Nevertheless, the meeting turned out to be a disaster. The pastor and his wife basically sided with my husband and his sister regarding their wanting to have frequent dining experiences without my knowledge of them! There is a lot more to this story that I will not be sharing in this book due to the nature of this matter!

Not once did they share a scripture about the responsibility of a husband putting his wife first or how family and outsiders should not overstep their boundaries. I felt more like a young girlfriend that day instead of a wife of almost forty years! I remember leaving and sobbing in my car. The pain from that day can still surface at times if I allow it to. I begin to think about all of the people that probably had experienced something very similar while members of a church.

The pain was very deep. I felt on some level; my husband had betrayed me instead of covering me as his wife. However, it was not the first time I had to defend myself as a wife, but it was the first time I had experienced church hurt on this level.

I shared my thoughts with my husband and told him that I was not going back to that church ever again! We both agreed that the ministry was not a good "fit" for our family and subsequently sent a formal letter to the ministry to let them know! Many may wonder why I would share something so personal in this book but due to the serious trauma from this incident, I feel the need to let others know that sometimes even people very close to you can wound you and the trauma from it may be lasting and may take years of healing.

SPIRITUAL TRAUMA A/K/A "CHURCH HURT"

Since writing this book, I have realized that spiritual trauma is one of the most overlooked problems in the church! I came across an incredible clinical therapist and pastor who realized the same.

Timothy Lane is the creator of God Therapy, a seven-step inner healing and deliverance model. Mr. Lane realized there was a void of understanding and addressing trauma in the church. He has done major work in the area of healing from church trauma by introducing the church world to his pioneered model of healing trauma through God Therapy.

Timothy Lane's book, *Healing Trauma God's Way*,[1] is a masterpiece that explains the marrying of inner healing, deliverance and therapeutic techniques and how all are connected and needed when addressing church trauma. He explains the importance of knowing when clinical modalities are needed versus spiritual deliverance. Mr. Lane believes the church can no longer hide the need to be trauma informed, trauma trained and to have ministries designed to heal those suffering from trauma. I totally agree with him and elated that he is sharing this!

One thing I absolutely love that Mr. Lane believes is that there are a lot of Christians who are "demonized" because they have been traumatized. Even though they have a relationship with Christ, they are still suffering emotional and mental damage from something that happened to them in their past. He further states that they are "worshipping while wounded and dancing while damaged!"

When it comes to church trauma, or any type of trauma for that matter, the worst thing a person can do is to ignore, numb, suppress or try and avoid their feelings. Avoidance is also a coping mechanism that many use in order not to address the emotional wounds and sadness that they are feeling. God created us with emotions for a reason. An important part of releasing painful emotions is allowing ourselves to feel them and express them.

As humans, we tend to either avoid or totally block out painful experiences altogether. Again, our bodies naturally make us numb to protect us from the pain. When this happens, it does not mean that the pain is no longer there. Instead, we have simply disconnected from it.

Even after experiencing church trauma or hurt, it is important to not isolate and find a way to re-connect with a local church or a safe, supportive community. Churches, Christian support groups and congregations play a significant role in offering a haven for trauma survivors. They all help to provide a sense of understanding, support, and guidance in the healing journey.

Questions for Reflection:

THOUGHTS:
After reading this chapter, do you think you have ever been hurt by the church or a spiritual community?

FEELINGS:

What are you feeling in your body after reading this chapter about spiritual trauma?

BEHAVIOR:

What, if anything, might you change about your life after reading this chapter?

CHAPTER [8]
How Grief, Trauma, and Emotional Pain are Connected

Grief has a mind of its own. Grief cannot be explained in one sentence. Grief can be mysterious and, at times, complicated. Grief is unique, and everyone's grief journey looks different. Grief is a process everyone will go through after experiencing a significant loss. Grief can transform us because of its immediate and physical impact. It can cause people who have never really acknowledged their emotions to have *to feel*. There is no such thing as "normal grief" because nothing is normal about grief, and nothing is constant in the grief process.

Sometimes things feel like they are moving at the speed of lightning when you are grieving. Oher times, it appears time has stopped altogether! One thing I have learned for sure is that there is no one way to grieve.

To date, I have been on some kind of grief journey for over thirty years. I say this because grief is not linear. There is no pattern or algorithm. When our first child died suddenly, my life changed forever. Prior to this event, no one close to me had died. My grandfather died a few days before we ever got to meet him. While this affected me and made me a little sad, it was not nearly the same level of grief and trauma that hit me after the death of my four-year-old son, our firstborn child!

Before I get ahead of myself, let me first define grief. Grief is a collection of strong and often very painful feelings that follow a loss of some kind. Basically, it is the emotional response to losing something or someone you care about deeply. Grief can be triggered by so many things and normally happens at the most inopportune time. I have shared with some people to think of recurring grief, especially during their deceased loved one's birthday, death anniversary, etc., as "lots of tiny paper cuts" because although it has been a little while since their death…it still hurts really, really bad!

Before I share about my grief journey after losing two of our children, I want you to understand just how powerful of a force grief is. Similar to death, it leaves us with so many unanswered questions. The human side of us longs for answers—answers to things that the human mind does not have privy to. This is when we must rely on our faith to give us solace and peace. Grief can become complicated when we try and manage it by living in denial. I always encourage people to cry if they feel they need to cry because suppressing our feelings and emotions during the grief process will not serve us well.

Grief is typically conceptualized as a reaction to a death of someone we love or deeply care about. Grief is also associated with any type of loss or when reality is not what we wanted, hoped for or even expected. This might be the loss of a job, a career, a friendship, a relationship, a home or any sentimental entity that was close to our heart.

In 1969 when Elisabeth Kübler-Ross wrote *On Death and Dying*, she introduced us to the five stages of grief. Persistent, traumatic grief can cause us to cycle, and at different times, through these various stages of grief. Here are the original five stages of grief, with the additional sixth stage introduced by David Kessler later on:

- **Denial** – This initial stage involves refusing to accept the reality of the loss, often characterized by disbelief and shock.

- **Anger** – As time passes and the reality of the loss sinks in, anger may emerge. This stage can overlap with other stages for a while.

- **Bargaining** – In this stage, individuals may try to negotiate with a higher power or fate to undo the loss, often driven by feelings of guilt of not having done enough.

- **Depression** – This is where intense sadness, despair, hopelessness and the full impact of loss is felt.

- **Acceptance** – Acceptance does not necessarily mean that one is "over" the loss, but it is a coming to terms with it and finding a way to live with and through it.

- **Finding Meaning/Moving On** – David Kessler introduced a sixth stage in his book, *Finding Meaning: The Sixth Stage of Grief*. This stage encompasses that beyond acceptance, bereaved individuals may find purpose and healing by searching for meaning in the loss.

These stages may not look the same for everyone, and some people may not go through all of these stages. Others may go through the stages at different times in their life after their loss or losses. Personally, I stayed in "denial" for almost one year after the death of my second child (my 32-year-old son). I just could not believe God would allow this to happen…again! I had a very difficult time accepting my son was gone forever.

During that first year, I would catch myself looking at my phone hoping he would call, and that this nightmare would end, but, of course, that never happened. Eventually, I had to accept there would be no more calls, family dinners, cookouts or beach trips with him.

One important thing I want everyone to know about grief is that there really is "No Expiration Date" for when your grief process will end. Even as I write this book, my 32-year-old son has been dead now for over four years and just a few days ago I broke down crying thinking about his nieces and nephews and the fact that he will never get to hold them or laugh and play with them. This is just one example of a what I call a "grief moment," and there have been many!

It's so important we realize that there is no end to grief, and I totally agree with grief expert David Kessler who says when people ask you "How long will you grieve for your wife, sister or your husband," he always says, "Well, how long is that person going to be dead?" He says, "If they're going to be dead for a long time, you're going to grieve for a long time." But that does not mean you will always be grieving in pain.

All I know is "complete closure" or "total healing" after a painful loss is unrealistic and may even be unhealthy because we are setting ourselves for some sort of false healing. I can clearly attest to the fact that grief comes in "waves" and some of the waves are big, some are huge, some are smooth and some are very rough.

It doesn't matter whether it's been twenty days or twenty years—something can trigger you to start thinking about your loved one and tears overtake you. The most important thing I want you to know is that it is okay "not to be okay" some days. Stop trying to prove to others that you are stronger than you really are. This may come back to haunt you. I know because it happened to me.

No human will ever conquer or fully understand the grief process. Nor will we be able to stop humans from dying, understand why babies get cancer, why natural disasters happen in some places and not others and the list goes on. When it comes to grief, you must give yourself permission to feel and process your grief.

It does not matter how many degrees and credentials a person has when it comes to the grief process. David Kessler, who again founded the sixth stage of grief, had his own experience with the grief process when his twenty-seven-old son died tragically. He writes, "After all my experience working with grief, a few years ago, my younger son died, accidentally and out of the blue." He recounts, "And you know, it was just brutal. I found myself wanting to write a note to everyone I had counseled, saying, 'I forgot how bad the pain is.'"

> When it comes to grief, you must give yourself permission to feel and process your grief.

Kessler went on to say that after working with hundreds of families who had lost loved ones, he saw how hard they searched for meaning. He stated that it did not matter whether the death occurred after a long, debilitating illness or if it came as a total shock after an accident. There is often a desire to see meaning in it.

I am convinced that it's difficult to find meaning without having "Hope!" The meaning does not have to be some huge thing or something that will put further financial strain on a family who may already be dealing with financial trauma as a result of the death. The meaning could be finding a cause that will honor your loved one. Meaning could be found in small moments that might produce big joy!

Our son Darius who died a few years ago worked a corporate job but loved music and would deejay part-time. His stage name was "DJ Ruler." He shared with me once that the name "DJ Ruler" was birthed out of a scripture (Exodus 18:21) that talked about men being "Men of good character because they were endowed with judicial laws." He felt that leaders were "Rulers," and he wanted to inspire people to "rule" with whatever gifts and abilities God had given them.

Some of our family's "finding meaning" out of DJ's death was when his older brother, our middle son, decided to carry on his brother's vision of promoting the "Ruler Mindset." He was always such an excellent role model to his younger brother and was always there for Darius no matter how much it cost him.

He has done an exceptional job and is the visionary behind establishing a scholarship endowment at Darius' alma mater, North Carolina A&T State University (Aggie Pride!). He and his wife, our sweet daughter-in-law, who is beyond brilliant, also coordinates an annual "Ruler Day" fundraiser on Darius's birthday, July 24th. There is an opportunity to donate to this wonderful movement in memory of our Darius by going to @djrulerforever on Instagram.

So many wonderful family and friends have supported this throughout the years, and some have even attended every year. This annual "Family and Friends" event has really helped our family to find some meaning in the passing of our sweet, incredibly kind son/brother. We will continue to bless young people with scholarships and share with them about DJ's values and desire to always help others before himself and to serve others every opportunity he got.

When looking at the stages of grief and how I navigated through each one, I must say that the one that gave me a massive amount of strength and joy was Stage Six – Finding Meaning/Moving On. It is important to feel that our loved one's life was not in vain and that they served a purpose here on earth. So, when it comes to what meaning is and what it is not in regards to grief, remember this:

- ✓ Meaning is relative and personal.
- ✓ Meaning takes time. You may not find meaning for months or for years after a loss.
- ✓ Meaning does not require understanding. Understanding is not necessary.
- ✓ Even when you do find meaning, you will not feel that it was worth the cost of what you lost.
- ✓ Your loss is not a test, a lesson or something to handle. It is not punishment.
- ✓ Only you can find your "meaning."
- ✓ Meaningful connections can heal painful memories.

It is important to understand the grief process because by getting more insight into this very complicated system, the more you will embrace healing in a different way. Sometimes, the unknown hinders our progress in ways that we are not even aware.

There are several types of grief, but I only want to focus on a few:

- ➢ **Complicated grief** – also known as "persistent complex bereavement disorder," complicated grief is defined as persistent feelings of sadness that cause functional impairment for at least a year after a loss.

- ➢ **Delayed grief** – is a type of complicated grief where the bereaved person doesn't experience the full impact of their loss immediately, but rather at a later point in time. Delayed grief is normally postponed or suppressed, with the person

> **Disenfranchised grief** – this occurs when a loss is not acknowledged or recognized by society, leading to feelings of isolation and difficulty in grieving.

> **Cumulative grief** – happens when you experience a second loss shortly after (or while you're still processing grief) from a first loss.

> **Collective grief** – happens when a tragedy affects an entire community or large group. Also seen after the death of a beloved public figure or a terrorist attack, after a mass casualty, or when a national tragedy occurs.

> **Absent grief** – means an individual is not showing any of the typical signs of grief. They may act as though they haven't experienced a loss at all. It can happen due to complete shock or total denial, and it's seen a lot in cases where a loss is sudden or unexpected.

So how is grief, trauma and emotional pain all connected? For starters, individuals experience all three of these if significant loss occurs. One does not necessarily have to happen for you to experience the others. All of them together can cause a cumulative effect. The ongoing stress and adversity needs to be closely managed. Grief is a natural response to loss, while trauma is a response to a sudden, distressing event, and the two can be closely related when a loss occurs in a traumatic way.

It is important to note, not all grief involves trauma, but a traumatic loss can heavily influence the grief experience. One very important fact to remember is grief is considered a natural response to loss, while trauma is a response to a highly stressful or shocking event. Both grief and trauma can contribute to mental health issues like PTSD, depression, anxiety, dissociation and many more, especially if the grief is complicated by a traumatic event.

Emotional pain comes into play with both grief and trauma. The main difference between pain and trauma is how someone heals after a difficult life event. When you experience a serious threat to your life, whether that is health-related or in regard to your emotional well-being, if you can cope with it, it may not be considered traumatic.

While emotional pain is something we experience in normal life situations, we are more prone to hurt and sensitivities when going from grief and trauma. It is important to find effective coping skills or practice more self-care routines than you normally do in order to deal with the additional emotional pain that comes with grief and trauma.

So many people do not realize the importance of healthy grieving. Studies have shown a big correlation between addiction and grief. If a person is grieving the death of a loved one while going through recovery, they are being challenged on a level that most cannot relate to. While they may have coped with stressors through substance abuse, they are now sober and may struggle to resist the temptation to revert to their old behavior.

Grief definitely stirs up addiction triggers. Addiction triggers are emotions and memories that lead to an impulse to use a substance or participate in some other form of addiction. Triggers do not necessarily result in relapse, but they may make it difficult to resist the urge to use drugs, alcohol or participate in addictive behavior. Here are a few healthy ways to cope with loss during addiction and also manage grief during recovery:

- ➢ **Let yourself grieve** – An important first step in grief management is to acknowledge it. When we try to bottle up feelings of loss, anger and sadness, that suppression only delays and lengthens your grieving process.

- ➢ **Reach out to your support system and do not isolate** – So many people feel the need to isolate when grieving which is not always helpful. While it is understandable to want some alone time, cutting yourself off from your support system is more likely to lead to relapse.

- ➢ **Stick to your treatment plan** – Although it may be a little more taxing, try to stick to the steps and management strategies set forth by your treatment program. Talk to your sponsor or counselor about what you are experiencing.

- ➢ **Maintain a routine of healthy activities** – In deep grief, people will sometimes forget to perform basic hygiene and personal care like brushing teeth, taking showers, staying hydrated and the like. Set reminders if necessary.

As much as I would like to forget the details of our two children dying and the traumatic events surrounding both of their deaths, this is not possible! That's the reality of trauma and how it affects you one way or another for the remainder of your life. When our four-year-old son died, I remember walking into the funeral home on the eve of his homegoing celebration. I remember how dark and serene it was until I walked up to my baby's casket and began to scream at the top of my lungs for them to "Turn the lights on…turn the lights on!" because he did not like being in the dark! Again, it's been over thirty years, and I am crying as I type this. This is the reality of grief, and I really want people to understand that it's okay if grief revisits as an uninvited guest, because it will whether you allow it to or not.

The months following the death of our first child were lonely for me. My husband was active duty Army at the time and had to go back to work. So, I was left to hold my eight-month-old baby boy most of the day. When I look back on it now, this was cathartic! I honestly do not think I would have made it if I had not had my sweet eight-month-old baby boy. He was my lifeline during this difficult and painful time. I remember making sure that he was well taken care of, and I did not take my eyes off of him, not even for a second.

My grieving process was so grueling because fear had arrested me, and as much I needed some self-care time, the thought of losing another one of my babies gripped me tighter than a paratrooper holding the risers of the parachute after jumping out of the plane.

I could see pounds slowly slipping off my body due to my not having an appetite. This was the first sign of what would be a long bout with "functional depression." For anyone who has never heard of this term, functional depression is a form of depression where individuals experience significant depressive symptoms but maintain their daily functioning and social roles. This would be my M.O. for a long while until I felt that I had healed enough to move forward.

The grief process for me after the loss of our first child was filled with a lot of indecisiveness and low energy. Both my husband and I had to force ourselves to do small outdoor activities just so the baby could get some fresh air. As much as we wanted things to go back to normal, we knew that our lives would never be "normal" again.

Finally, we decided to go to Virginia Beach to visit some close friends who we had met while living in Germany. They had called us several times and insisted that we get away from the familiar, and boy were they right! Just going to sit by the ocean was incredible and we felt a spiritual connection to Erran, our sweet four-year-old who had died. This is why I encourage people I now counsel or coach to take a short sabbatical after a traumatic event or death of someone close to them. It's almost like a getting away to come back to a "new normal" that will never be normal.

For those parents who have lost children and are reading this book, I am not sure that we as parents ever stop grieving or missing our babies. It is just too unnatural to comprehend them leaving this Earth before us. Grief and death are the mysteries of life that we will only understand to a certain degree. I believe only our Creator has the answers to this test, and all we can do is trust him for the results.

As with trauma, grief has its own unique look. Depending on the circumstances and depending on the individual, grief can look very different. Here are a few scenarios where grief is the culprit behind their behavior:

- Sarah works two 12-hour shifts as a nurse to cope with her ongoing grief
- Jim fishes three days a week versus one like he used to
- James awakens at 2:00 a.m. nightly; watches television for hours and then is exhausted at work the next day
- Kim stays in bed until noon and used to be an early riser
- Mark is constantly irritable for no reason
- Jean cleans the house for hours every single day
- Bobby forgot to shower for days on end
- Zachary watches television all day and all night

- Destiny looks normal but cries into her pillow every night
- Darnell washes, cleans or waxes his car daily
- Gina eats at five-star restaurants as therapy

I am certain that we could add many more scenarios, but the point is taken…grief looks different on everyone, and everyone's grief process is unique to them—much like their fingerprints.

Finally, there are few things that we should never say to someone who has lost a loved one, especially a child:

- **I know how you feel.** – You absolutely DO NOT know unless you have experienced a similar loss and even then, everyone's grief process looks different

- **Time will heal all pain.** – Time does not heal; time soothes or makes the pain more bearable

- **This happened for a reason.** – And unless you have the reason, say less!

- **You'll get over this.** – How do you know?

- **Don't cry!** – Should I smile instead?

Questions for Reflection:

THOUGHTS:
After reading this chapter, how do you think your grief, trauma, and emotional pain might be interconnected?

FEELINGS:

What are you feeling in your body after reading this chapter?

BEHAVIOR:

What, if anything, might you change about your life after reading this chapter?

CHAPTER [9]
The Pandemic of 2020 & How Trauma Manifested

We should have known a year with two of the same numbers in it (2020) was going to be different! But, we never could have known how different and anxiety-provoking it would be! Prior to the pandemic, trauma was in the shadows. People knew about it, sure, but no one felt a need to really talk about it. But ALL of that changed in the blink of an eye in 2020!

The pandemic was the "Great Equalizer" because for the first time everyone was experiencing anxiety, confusion and fear of the unknown at the same time. We were not able to hide our feelings as easily as we had before. And, we were all vulnerable. Everyone feared the unknown, and their anxiety was proof of it. Everyone was feeling the stress of the pandemic. Like, what is a "quarantine" anyway? I had never really heard this word, and I was almost sixty years old at stage time!

There were missed graduations, missed birthday parties, missed funerals of loved ones, missed births of children and grandchildren, stay-at-home orders, furloughs, job loss, masking, closed stores and malls, protests and a slew of other stuff. The pandemic caused people's anxiety to go through the roof! It was indeed a very stressful time for the entire world! The emotional exhaustion had never been at this level.

The pandemic put us in a serious chokehold, and even when it finally decided to release us…it attempted to drag us all the way down the street and into a cold, dark alley!

The pandemic of 2020 will have lasting effects not only on families but on marriages and relationships too. The American Family Survey (AFS) study suggested that the pandemic increased stress and tension in millions of relationships. Couples who were hardly communicating were suddenly forced into an "in-home" date night!

The pandemic was definitely not all bad. It caused people to take a long hard look at life from the perspective of what we can control as humans and what is providence and something that only God has control of! The entire experience was absolutely mind-blowing to me because we were taught so many lessons in what looked like one session!

Lessons such as:

- ✓ Family time is sacred and should not be neglected
- ✓ Peace of mind is more valuable than money or things
- ✓ Health is one of our greatest assets
- ✓ We can survive on so much less when necessary
- ✓ Stop sweating the small stuff, and everything might be small
- ✓ Church is not just a building but a heart posture
- ✓ Keep the "main things" the Main Thang!
- ✓ Focus on the present moment…not the problems!

THE PANDEMIC OF 2020 & HOW TRAUMA MANIFESTED

There are so many more lessons that could be added to this list and some may not even be evident yet. The things that really concerned me were mostly related to mental health issues because I was about to finish graduate school with a master's degree in Marriage and Family Therapy for counseling and would not be able to use it for a long while. At least, not at the level that I had anticipated.

As I stated, the year 2020 hit differently for me. I had decided one year prior to this, in 2019, to go back to graduate school after being out of college for over twenty (20) years! I was fifty-eight years old at the time and had stopped pursuing most of my dreams in order to raise our two sons. My children were always my top priority after God and my husband. I remember turning down high-paying jobs with the Department of Defense because they would have required me to be out-of-town a lot and not there to support my young sons. I decided being a mother to my children was an assignment from God that I took so seriously, and boy did it pay off! Both of them ending up graduating from college (with honors) and neither has ever disappointed us or made us regret the sacrifices that we made for them.

Even as I write this sentence, my eyes are watering as I think about how they tried to make us proud parents by accomplishing what we sent them to college to do! So, setting my dreams aside was a no-brainer when it came to our children. I felt that I would know when the time was right to begin pursuing my dreams and the proof would be in the peace that would follow.

So there I was, January 2020, in my last semester of a sixteen-month accelerated master's counseling programs that was beyond hard on so many levels that I still cannot articulate it. It was one of only two programs like it in the country. The U.S. Army had created this program for active duty chaplains who would become Brigade chaplains (a military term that meant they would be spiritual advisors to hundreds and maybe thousands of soldiers one day).

It just so happened that I applied to the university that the U.S. Army had selected to do a pilot program with and were allowing a few citizens to apply for the program and be in the cohort as well. I had no idea that I was making history as only the second citizen to be accepted into the program. When I look back, only God himself helped me to finish that program and get through one of the toughest years of my life. I had no idea that the trauma training in this program was preparing me for the unimaginable!

The excitement that I had garnered from knowing that May 2020 was only a few months away had given me "new strength and hope" like never before. Little did I know that the year would turn out to be one of the most tragic and traumatic years of my life. Not only from having to adjust to isolation and quarantines, but from dealing with one unknown after another. What would begin as a year of total exhilaration knowing I would be graduating from a master's program that I could not even believe I had gotten accepted into (one of the requirements was that you could not be employed) to an anxiety-ridden year that would ultimately end with the sudden death of our second child!

I want to take you on my personal journey of my year during the pandemic by starting with an opportunity of a lifetime at the beginning of the year. In January 2020, I was beyond ecstatic to be asked to be on my very first nationally syndicated radio show where I shared about the reasons behind writing my first book, *Silenced By Arms…Children Are Dying*, which is based on the true story our first child, our four-year-old son, being accidentally shot by a young boy cousin and subsequently dying in my parents' bedroom.

THE PANDEMIC OF 2020 & HOW TRAUMA MANIFESTED

I had been waiting so long to finally be in the national spotlight and share my story about the importance of storing firearms/guns safely—far, far away from the little inquisitive hands and minds that may find them and lose their little lives in an instance.

So, getting an opportunity at the very beginning of the year had me so over-the-moon emotionally and gave me tremendous joy that the entire year would be one of my best. If I had just remembered how my life had panned out prior to this whenever I would get excited, I would have known better. History has shown me that every time I get really excited about something, my joy would be short-lived from either bad news or impending sorrow!

I decided to tuck these negative thoughts way back in the furthest place in my mind because I was still convinced that 2020 was the year of "Total Wins" for Roxie!

February rolled by and then March presented as a season of hope and anticipatory joy until around the middle of the month when, as we all know now, "all Hell broke loose." Everything shut down faster than air going out of an air mattress when an unsuspecting hole appears!

I will never forget walking into the building where our counseling program was and seeing everyone all huddled together. The looks on their faces were a mix of confusion, dismay and sadness. I wasn't sure what was going on. Upon inquiring, I learned that the center was being shut down until further notice and we all had to immediately get certified in telehealth counseling so we could still counsel our clients. Then everything started moving at what seemed like the speed of lightning!

The news stations were putting out information at a rate that I had never seen before. The sensory overload was just beginning and would continue for the next six to nine months. Although I was concerned about the health implications, I was more worried about all of us being able to graduate on time two months later! Our program guidelines were strict and everyone knew there couldn't be any breaks as far as instruction went or the student had to start all over again!

My eyes began to water as I thought about all the hard work and sacrifices that both me and my family had made in order for me to fulfill my lifelong dream of obtaining my master's degree. I was relieved when our supervisor informed us that we would still be able to graduate in May of 2020 as scheduled.

As the months ensued, I could see people fill with anxiety and nervousness as more and more people began to die from coronavirus complications. So many family members and friends were dying. The level of grief, sadness and hopelessness was unbelievable to say the least. Everyone it seemed was searching desperately for a touch of normalcy, but their search came up empty every time.

During the pandemic, I began to think of creative ways to keep our family connected so we could stay strong and rely on each other's strength to make it through. I texted my siblings and suggested we do a weekly prayer call so our eighty-five-year-old mother would not get ill from the stress. We were desperately trying to protect her because she was definitely in the high-risk group!

The month of May finally arrived, and we managed to have a virtual military graduation ceremony. Family members were able to attend the in-person ceremony, and masks were required to be worn at all times, except for when eating. I will be forever grateful that family members were able to join virtually, especially my 32-year-old youngest son. I had no idea that three months later he would die in a car accident. A year that was already a nightmare experience would get even worse within three months of my graduating from graduate school.

We managed to get through the summer by purchasing our very first above-ground pool. This was mostly for Sarah, our little seven-year-old daughter, who loves water but was unable to go to the local water park as she normally had. As the summer dwindled down and fall was fast approaching, we looked up and it was September, my all-time favorite month, my birth month and the month with the most beautiful weather (not too hot and not cold yet). We had survived six months of the pandemic and felt that we had found our rhythm. Little did we know that our family's rhythm was about to change again—and this time for life.

Sarah was excited because we had promised to take her to the beach Labor Day weekend, and she had not forgotten. I had worked really hard up until this point to keep her grounded and her emotions regulated. We wanted the trip to be our entire family, and our youngest son had actually planned to join us, but due to a series of events just hours prior to leaving, he decided to stay home and rest.

In hindsight, Darius had visible anxiety issues, and I could tell that something was not right. As a mother and as a trained mental health professional, I was picking up some very concerning vibes and, at one point, started to cancel the weekend getaway. The mother instinct was trying to tell me to "trust" what I was feeling, but because of the vast amount of stress, anxiety and emotional exhaustion, I felt I needed to experience the therapeutic benefit of the ocean probably more than all of them. I had just completed one of the most challenging master's programs and was unable to just go away alone and decompress.

Sitting on the beach really revitalized me. I am forever grateful for those twenty-four hours that would awaken my barren soul. The rest and relaxation were priceless because we would need every ounce of stored energy as we prepared to get the worst news again as parents—that another one of our children had died!

As I shared in the beginning of this book, after getting the call to return home immediately, I braced myself for bad news. My body had already begun to tense up and my nervous system was starting to become unregulated. After learning that our youngest son had gotten killed in a car accident, I felt like running away from home as an adult. The stress and trauma from the entire tragedy had sucked me into some dark, deep hole and I was fighting desperately to get out!

After laying our son to rest, I suggested that our immediate family take a short sabbatical so we could begin to process some of the unbelievable trauma. It was difficult to concentrate, and all of us were fighting to stay alive emotionally. The pandemic had already zapped most of the good energy out of us and now this tragedy would try to finish us off. Our family had endured other tragedies and several "near-death" experiences, so we were not new to this—but were most definitely "true to this!"

We were built to last and galvanized around each other so that when one would collapse from the emotional load, someone was there to help them get back up. Going through so much trauma in our family really has taught us that "family is forever" and God knew that we would need each other at various times in our lives.

One example I like to use during family counseling is to explain the Japanese art of kintsugi. Kintsugi is the art of repairing broken pottery by mending the areas that are broken with lacquer dusted with powdered gold, silver or platinum. This technique enhances the scars with precious metal instead of trying to hide them. I believe sometimes families try to hide their disabilities, their frailties and their problems in general. Every family has conflict and every family finds solutions!

The overarching message of kintsugi is to celebrate the broken pieces and not focus on the false idea of perfection! It's important to find beauty even in the damaged or imperfect parts that may come with being a human and a part of a family. Every family is unique and just like the art of kintsugi, the process takes a long time but afterwards, the pottery, no matter what it's been through, emerges stronger and more beautiful than before.

> Kintsugi is the art of repairing broken pottery by mending the areas that are broken with lacquer dusted with powdered gold, silver or platinum.

Although the devastation from the pandemic and the years that followed is yet to be seen, I believe it made us stronger in so many ways. I further believe that it could be years before the fallout emotionally, mentally, physically and spiritually manifests. The most important factor is to ask for support, continue to process and heal in healthy ways and learn the lessons that the pandemic tried to teach us.

We all know that traumatic events can leave us feeling shocked, hopeless, a little fearful and unable to cope. However, healing is a must because when trauma is not processed, it lingers! Sometimes, that lingering affects our nervous system and all the other systems as well. When trauma gets trapped in the body—it must be released eventually, or things will go from bad to worse fairly quickly.

Questions for Reflection:

THOUGHTS:
How was your life affected by the pandemic? Did any of your pain and trauma surface during that time?

FEELINGS:

What are you feeling in your body after reading this chapter?

BEHAVIOR:

What, if anything, might you change about your life after reading this chapter about the pandemic?

CHAPTER [10]
Womb Trauma: The Seed of Trauma

Trauma really can manifest in unthinkable ways! Could it be that even before we see the effects of trauma in the natural state that in so many cases it begins in the womb? While researching how trauma affects our bodies in more ways than we know, I started thinking about the fact that three months after losing our four-year-old child tragically, my husband and I conceived another baby. I would carry this baby in my womb while still grieving the death of our four-year-old.

I remember crying a lot during that pregnancy and feeling sad and depressed for months. Knowing what I know now, I seriously believe there is a correlation between these emotional cycles and the anxiety issues that our son had. Could all the womb stress have affected him?

"Womb Trauma" refers to the potential impact of a mother's traumatic experiences or stress during pregnancy on the developing fetus, leading to emotional and physiological effects that can very likely persist throughout life. This should not come as a surprise but can still be alarming. Doctors have always warned expecting mothers to slow down, not be stressed, to refrain from drinking alcohol or other harmful substances.

Trauma experienced by the mother will definitely affect the fetus when there have been cases of domestic violence, substance abuse or lack of prenatal care. This and so much more can show up later in the child as cognitive delay and various other developmental problems. Elevated stress hormones such as cortisol can cross the placenta and effect the fetus, and this is extremely troubling as well. Excessive exposure to stress hormones during pregnancy can lead to long-term health issues.

Womb trauma can actually be the culprit behind so many childhood anxiety and personality disorders and more studies need to be done so that children are given the support they need to thrive. It makes so much sense how womb trauma can contribute to a range of mental health challenges, including depression and even PTSD later in life due to nervous system of the small fetus being extremely sensitive.

Early trauma events can be encoded in the fetus's limbic system, potentially leading to difficulties with processing emotional regulation, memories, behavior, and learning or survival instincts.

When the womb is holding onto unresolved emotional pain, stress, or trauma, it can lead to chronic pain, inflammation, and disease in the body. This womb trauma phenomenon could be more widespread than we initially thought. The fact that when a mother gets pregnant and has unresolved emotional issues or unhealed trauma is a crucial element to her child's development.

> Early trauma events can be encoded in the fetus's limbic system, potentially leading to difficulties with processing emotional regulation, memories, behavior, and learning or survival instincts.

When I was carrying my second child right after the death of our four-year-old son, I wish that I had known more about womb trauma because it might have helped me in my healing journey. I would have concentrated more on regulating my emotions so that the baby would not be affected emotionally. I am hoping that by writing this book, more awareness on this subject will surface because this may be an overlooked health issue that warrants more attention.

I carried three babies to full term, but it was only the last baby where I can vividly remember being totally unregulated almost on a weekly basis. I remember crying profusely around Christmas after our first child died. That would have put me in the first trimester which is said to be the most crucial time of the pregnancy. This one evening in particular, I remember I had cried so long that my stomach started hurting and I called my doctor. He asked me the medical questions that I guess helped him to determine that the baby was not in danger. He also instructed me to call him back if the pains either got worse or continued into the next morning. I listened intensely, but it was what he said prior to hanging up that really had my body in full attention mode. He said, "Roxie, you just lost one of your babies, you are going to have to fight for your emotional healing if you want this baby to be healthy and thrive." I knew what he was saying.

My baby boy arrived seven months later. He was seven pounds and a few ounces and was not missing any limbs, fingers or toes. He was a tremendous blessing to our family, not to mention how super cute he was with his shiny jet black and curly hair—I mean lots and lots of hair! He was a little miracle and even smiled on day one!

As I think back, he seemed like a normal baby until around fifteen months. Then he began to cry what seemed like nonstop. I could not find one thing wrong with him, but we kept going back to the doctor's. I sincerely think they wanted to turn me away one day, but the entire office knew my story, so they were extremely compassionate and assisted me to the best of their abilities.

The only thing that soothed him was when he was picked up and held very closely. He would calm right down. Knowing what I know

now about regulation, I do believe that the baby needed to be held in order to feel safe. This could have been the beginning of what would be a foreshadowing of years to come. Sometimes, we just do not have all the answers, and we have to use the information that we do have and do the best we can.

The one thing that I do remember when I look at the personalities of both our sons, the one with the possible womb trauma was definitely more sensitive emotionally and had anxiety disorders that would show up at unexpected times, but he seemed to manage them very well. I made it a point as a mother to hug him very often and to make sure he was feeling loved because I could see that he needed a little extra reassurance. I did not see anger issues until a few years before his death. I believe life had thrown him some curveballs that made his anxiety worse. As a family, we could tell when something or someone had bothered him because his personality would change, and he would even get very quiet on occasions.

The more I learned about womb trauma, the more I pondered if I had done enough to protect my baby while he was in my womb. This inner struggle took me on deeper path of research and query. I found out about something called **"Broken heart syndrome,"** a popular topic of discussion in the past few years. Also called, "stress-induced cardiomyopathy," it typically occurs after a physical or emotional traumatic event, such as divorce, serious car accidents, loss of a loved one, fights, or near-drowning experiences.

According to cardiologist Dr. David O'Neil, the causes of Broken heart syndrome occurs when adrenaline and other stress hormones, such as epinephrine are released when we undergo a significant amount of stress. When this happens, our heart rates and blood pressure increases. In some cases, the heart is overwhelmed and damaged by this sudden and rapid stress. The heart muscle then weakens causing complications similar to heart failure.

WOMB TRAUMA: THE SEED OF TRAUMA

When I read about this, I immediately felt that this is what happened to me—twice! I had experienced this exact condition both times our children died. Many times I felt my heart racing, and as I look back, panic attacks were something that I dealt with frequently. Why is this relevant? Because all of it happened while my baby was inside my womb. The emotional bond that a mother has with her baby in the womb is not only an emotional bond but a physiological bond. So again, womb trauma warrants so much more research because of the serious mental health implications.

I've thought about other people who I knew who may had been affected by their womb experience and in two cases that I was aware of, the babies were exposed to drugs while in the womb. In one instance, the mother had addictive behavior and had not just used drugs but never sought prenatal care for the entire nine months of her pregnancy. Her baby experienced what we would call "withdrawal symptoms" and has shown other developmental issues as well. Again, womb trauma can have long lasting effects, and the extent of the damage may never be fully discovered.

Drugs are not the only culprits that can contribute to womb trauma. Many babies are born with "Fetal Alcohol Syndrome" which can cause lots of developmental problems in children as well. The impairments of Fetal Alcohol Syndrome are serious.

Also, referred to as Fetal Alcohol Spectrum Disorder (FASD), this is a lifelong disability caused by exposure to alcohol in the womb. Alcohol passes through the placenta and is absorbed by the developing fetus, interfering with brain and organ development. The impact of alcohol is dependent upon frequency, amount and timing (at which stage was the alcohol consumed).

There could be a host of other things that could affect the fetus, such as the expectant mother experiencing physical, emotional or psychological abuse and so much more. Let's continue to get more educated and informed about this all-important topic so our children can enjoy healthy, thriving lives.

Questions for Reflection:

THOUGHTS:
Have you ever heard of the term "womb trauma" before? What did you learn reading this chapter?

FEELINGS:

What are you feeling in your body after reading this chapter?

BEHAVIOR:

What, if anything, might you change about your life after reading this chapter?

CHAPTER [11]
Trauma in the Workplace

There is so much research about trauma that it would take a few series of books to share it all! The topic of trauma and how it affects us is vast and complex. A topic like trauma literally touches every aspect of our lives and is definitely worth millions of dollars of research. I reiterate, just the fact that "womb trauma" is extremely serious and can impact the socio-economic and psychological canvas of our country—should be enough to make the decision-makers stop and take note!

Researchers are saying a lot about trauma. They recognize that trauma, particularly childhood trauma, has profound and lasting effects on brain development, mental and physical health, on marriages and families and overall well-being with potential for both negative and positive outcomes.

Trauma is not something that can be left at home when a person goes to work. Therefore, an employee with "unhealed trauma" can and will affect the culture in the workplace. The arguments, disagreements, prejudices and other conflict that arise in some workplace environments can possibly be either directly or indirectly related to trauma! Some of the anxiety and trauma that we see in the workplace could also be attributed to the type of leadership model in use. If there are individuals who are micromanaging their teams—this can cause the environment to be anxiety-provoking and less productive.

Research has shown that companies perform better when leaders empower, encourage, and coach employees instead of delivering orders, micromanaging, and giving out unwarranted discipline. At the root of these issues, the tendency to micromanage stems from a leader's own anxiety and lack of confidence. In order to break this unhealthy cycle of management, leaders should look inward to understand what is causing them to act this way. The majority of time, it is impossible to satisfy a micromanager! Micromanaging others is often a response to "unhealed trauma" and/or trust issues!

It is inherently naïve for companies to think that employees with a history of trauma will not affect their bottom lines! So, it would serve corporations well to invest in trauma management training. Employee productivity and overall well-being should always be a top priority in every corporation or company. This overarching subject of trauma management transcends the workplace and can be applied to all of our relationships. The recent spotlights on work-life balance are all the more reason for employees to take their unhealed trauma dilemmas more seriously. Work-life balance refers to achieving a harmonious equilibrium between professional and personal life, encompassing family, hobbies, self-care, and overall well-being. A good work-life balance is crucial for both personal and professional wellness. It can lead to increased productivity, reduced stress, improved physical and mental health, and enhanced social connections.

In order to identify which workplace behaviors are stemming from unhealed trauma, step one is to understand the serious dynamics of unhealed trauma. In this chapter, I will share some final statistics about how trauma affects every area of our lives—even in the workplace! Studies have shown that 70% of adults have some form of past trauma. When that trauma is unhealed or has gone unchecked, we often have disproportionate reactions in the workplace to triggered emotions.

Recent studies reveal the importance of healing from trauma. Harvard studies revealed that individuals who actively engage in healing their past traumas are 60% more likely to achieve long-term happiness and success. By making this mindset shift and addressing and healing old trauma wounds, you can shift your mindset, build resilience and create brighter, more positive futures; it ripples out!

> Trauma is not something that can be left at home when a person goes to work. Therefore, an employee with "unhealed trauma" can and will affect the culture in the workplace.

Researchers are encouraging individuals to stop using avoidance as their healing modality. Monitoring emotional triggers is not only about finding a "quick fix" and avoiding discomfort—it is more about understanding the patterns that keep showing up in your life. Become more self-aware of how often something triggers you and how intense that reaction feels and then how long it lingers in your heart and mind.

True healing begins when we acknowledge our pain and commit to transforming it into strength. We cannot allow past pain to dictate and control our present and future plans. Researchers are discovering more and more ways to heal from trauma.

People are getting intentional about their self-care and really getting in tune with their emotions instead of ignoring what is going on inside their bodies. Things such as unresolved pain and triggers can just appear out of nowhere, but in actuality they are rooted in deeper wounds. Studies show that repetitive triggers are often linked to unmet needs of past traumas.

You can start by asking yourself, "What is this emotion?" or "What is this feeling trying to tell me?" Your body may have an answer for you! Or, "How can I handle it differently the next time I feel this way?" Trauma has a story that it is trying to tell, but it is up to us to choose which version gets told. Healing starts with choosing positivity and support. It starts with having an honest conversation with yourself!

Researchers state that true healing happens when we stop reacting blindly and start responding **intentionally**! If the same trigger keeps showing up, it's an opportunity to shift something inside ourselves. Emotional growth is about recognizing the patterns and reframing the narratives, so it no longer controls us. Healing is not the absence of a trigger; it's the mastery of it.

I mentioned earlier in this book that the number one way most individuals cope with their unhealed trauma is by avoidance. There has been research to support this theory. Some evidence suggests it may be possible to block something such as an unwanted memory. When an unwanted memory intrudes the mind, it is a natural human reaction to want to block it out. More than a century ago, Sigmund Freud noted that humans have a defense mechanism that they use to help manage and block traumatic experiences and unwanted memories.

Many studies have shown that the suffering from trauma cannot be measured, yet it is literally encoded into our brains. Studies using neuroimaging have demonstrated which brain systems play a part in deliberate forgetting, and several studies have shown that it is possible for people to deliberately block memories from their consciousness.

Before we delve into all the different ways people use techniques to forget unwanted memories, I believe it's important to explain how memories are formed. Neurons are nervous system cells that use electrical impulses and chemical signals to transmit information not just to the brain but throughout the body. The brain contains approximately *86 billion neurons*, and each can form and connect to other neurons, potentially creating up to *1,000 trillion* connections!

Many experts define memory as how the mind interprets, stores, and retrieves information. Memories develop when a person processes an event, causing neurons to send signals to each other, creating a network of connections of various strength. What's interesting about the memory process is the more a person dwells on a memory, the stronger these neuronal connections become. Memories typically remain as long as a person revisits them. When a person revisits a memory, it becomes flexible again. The memory either weakens or get stronger and more vivid with each recall.

Experts refer to this process of strengthening as reconsolidation. This process can alter memories and can impact them either positively or negatively.

Most scientists agree there are four different types of memory:

- ❖ Working memory
- ❖ Sensory memory
- ❖ Short-term memory
- ❖ Long-term memory

Working memory is a type of memory that involves the immediate and small amount of information that a person actively uses as they perform cognitive tasks. **Sensory memory** allows you to remember sensory information after the stimulation has ended. It helps you to remember the sensation of a person's touch or a sound you heard in passing. **Short-term memory**, as the name implies, allows you to recall specific information about something for a brief period of time.

The memory where trauma resides is **long-term memory**. This is where we store a vast majority of our memories. Any memory we can recall after 30 seconds could be classified as long-term memory. There is no limit to how much our long-term memory can hold and for how long. We can further split long-term memory into two main categories: explicit and implicit long-term memory.

Explicit long-term memories are memories we consciously and deliberately take time to form and recall. It often includes major milestones in your life, such as childhood events, graduation dates and events or academic work learned in school. We are often not as deliberate with forming implicit memories as we are with explicit ones. Implicit memories form unconsciously and may affect the way a person thinks and behaves.

A person is using implicit memory when they learn motor skills like walking or riding a bike. If you learned how to ride a bike when you were eight years old and did not pick it up again until you are 18, implicit memory helps you remember how to ride it. Allow me to add here that different areas of the brain also specialize in storing different types of memories. While no single region of the brain stores all memories, the hippocampus plays a crucial role in forming and organizing new memories, especially those related to events and facts, and then it transfers them to other areas of the brain for long-term storage, like the neocortex. The neocortex holds long-term episodic memories, which are memories of specific events.

The amygdala, which is part of the limbic system, is involved in processing emotional memories, particularly those related to fear, strong emotions and trauma. The amygdala is the small, almond-shaped structure in the brain that plays a very important role when it comes to trauma. The amygdala is where emotions are processed, including fear and anxiety.

To explain a little further, when someone experiences a traumatic event, the amygdala becomes highly active, leading to the release of stress hormones and the activation of the "fight-or-flight" response. When individual with PTSD (Post-Traumatic Stress Disorder) are exposed to trauma-related triggers, the amygdala can actually react as if the trauma is happening again, leading to panic attacks, flashbacks, disorientation and other symptoms we well.

Memory plays such an important role in trauma healing. It is a very important variable because it is at the root of the trauma experience. Some evidence supports the theory of motivated forgetting. This theory suggests that people can block unpleasant, painful or traumatic memories if there is a motivation to do so. I have used this myself and believe that the majority of individuals are using this to cope with their trauma instead of going to therapy to process the traumatic events.

People have become very strategic in finding ways to cope with their childhood trauma and unhealed adult trauma. Some people have used thought or memory substitution strategies to help them suppress unwanted memories. This technique suggests that people can and have substituted a negative memory by redirecting their consciousness toward an alternative memory. Experts sometimes describe this unique technique as what happens when a person slams on the brakes in a car or steers to avoid a hazard.

We see a lot of redirecting of memories with individuals diagnosed with PTSD. Research continues to reveal how trauma and PTSD change the brain in four specific ways. When trapped in a constant trauma response people with PTSD experience four types of difficult PTSD symptoms to include:

- ❖ Painful thoughts
- ❖ Intense emotions
- ❖ Bodily changes
- ❖ Behavioral changes

Traumatic experiences like abuse, assault, or witnessing violence or tragedy can leave someone feeling constantly on edge. PTSD can impact your emotions, your stability, and can impact your relationships.

It is believed once we understand how trauma impacts the brain and our emotions that many symptoms can be reversed. Healing is possible when traumatic events are properly processed. Research has helped us to understand the vital role that our emotions play in keeping us grounded as humans. Emotions are a powerful form of communication. However, what we have learned in our society is not how to work with our emotions, but how to block and avoid them. All of this must change NOW if we are to truly start healing from trauma!

Symptoms like anxiety and depression are seriously on the rise in the United States and can stem from the way we are dealing with our unhealed trauma and our hard-wired survival emotions, which are the biological forces that should not be ignored.

Current research and neuroscientists suggest that the more stress, emotions and conflicts a person experiences, the more anxiety they can feel. This is due in part, to the vagus nerve, which is one of the main emotional centers in the body.[1]

Emotional stress, like that from blocked emotions, has not only been linked to mental illness, but also to physical problems like heart disease, intestinal problems, headaches, inflammation, insomnia, autoimmune disorders and more.

High levels of stress can lead to increased blood pressure, higher heart rate, elevated blood sugar and increased fat in the blood, all of which can strain the kidneys and potentially lead to kidney damage. While we all realize that some stress is normal and cannot be avoided, chronic stress can lead to a sustained "fight-or-flight" response, which causes the body to work harder to maintain health.

To bring this topic of the seriousness of stress on the body, allow me to share some statistics that many may not be aware of. According to the National Kidney Foundation (2024) fact sheet:

> ➤ Kidney disease, also known as "chronic kidney disease" (CKD), causes more deaths each year than breast cancer or prostate cancer. It is the under-recognized public health crisis.

> ➤ About 9 in 10 (90%) adults with kidney disease do not know they have it.

> ➤ About 1 in 3 (40%) of adults with severe kidney disease do not know they have it.

> ➤ Adults with kidney disease are at a higher risk of early death.

One thing that all researchers and scientists tend to agree on when talking about trauma is the amount of **stress** that it puts on the mind, body and spirit. Stress puts an emotional toll on the body and can cause the body to hold the nervous system hostage by holding onto the trauma that is being stored.

Stress is nothing to play with when it comes to our health. I am not sure that everyone still realizes just how much unhealed trauma plays a part in whether you are living a stressed or a peaceful life! If I may use a quintessential analogy…I sincerely believe that stress and trauma are first cousins!

Stress tends to show up in a number of ways. Here are just a few common effects of stress and how they can affect your body and behavior, according to the Mayo Clinic.

Stress symptoms may be affecting your health, even though you might not know it. You may blame sickness for that annoying headache, your sleeping troubles, feeling unwell or your lack of focus at work. But stress from workplace trauma may really be the cause.

COMMON EFFECTS OF STRESS

Stress symptoms can affect your body, your thoughts and feelings, and your behavior. Knowing common stress symptoms can help you manage them. Stress that's not dealt with can lead to many health problems, such as high blood pressure, heart disease, stroke, obesity and diabetes.

On your body	On your mood	On your behavior
Headache	Anxiety	Overeating or undereating
Muscle tension or pain	Restlessness	Angry outbursts
Chest pain	Lack of motivation or focus	Drug or alcohol misuse

On your body	On your mood	On your behavior
Fatigue	Memory problems	Tobacco use
Change in sex drive	Feeling overwhelmed	Avoiding friends and staying at home
Stomach upset	Grumpiness or anger	Exercising less often
Sleep problems	Sadness or depression	
Getting sick easier due to a weaker immune system		

ACTIONS TO MANAGE STRESS

If you have stress symptoms, taking steps to manage your stress can have many health benefits. Check out many possible stress management tips.

For example:

- Get regular physical activity on a weekly basis.
- Practice relaxation techniques. Try deep breathing, meditation, yoga, or massages.
- Make self-care a priority.
- Spend time with family and friends.
- Set aside time for hobbies. Read a book, listen to music or go for a walk. Schedule time for your passions.
- Write in a journal.
- Get enough sleep.
- Eat a healthy, balanced diet.
- Stay away from/do not use illegal substances.

Source (Mayo Clinic)

Aim to find active ways to manage your stress. Idle ways to manage stress that don't get you moving may seem relaxing. But they may make your stress go up over time. Examples are watching television, going on the internet or playing video games.

WHEN TO ASK FOR HELP!

If you're not sure if stress is the cause, or if you've taken steps to control your stress but you keep having symptoms, see your health care provider. Your health care provider may want to check for other potential causes. Or think about seeing a counselor or therapist, who can help you find the sources of your stress and learn new coping tools. And if you are concerned about harming yourself, call 911 or a suicide hotline.

Also, get emergency help right away if you have chest pain, especially if you also have shortness of breath; jaw, back, shoulder or arm pain; sweating; dizziness; or nausea. These may be warning signs of a heart attack and not simply stress symptoms.

To conclude, trauma in the workplace should be taken seriously and we can look at past events where employees went to their companies and killed innocent people. Quite possibly from unmanaged or un-diagnosed mental health issues or some other traumatic dilemma that may have started in the workplace.

Questions for Reflection:

THOUGHTS:

After reading this chapter, do you think you have ever experienced trauma in the workplace? How were you affected?

FEELINGS:

What are you feeling in your body after reading this chapter?

BEHAVIOR:

What, if anything, might you change about your life after reading this chapter?

CHAPTER [12]
Choosing Healing: Getting Help and Getting Whole!

I never thought in a million years that trauma would chase me as it has! I sincerely believe God has written my life story and has equipped me to share it, even as additional chapters are surfacing!

Had I known how "unhealed trauma wounds" would ultimately sabotage my life for years, I would have gone to therapy sooner. I would have gone to more anger management classes, and I definitely would have taken my healing more seriously. I have written this book to encourage and challenge you to start walking your own path towards healing.

> Life is a beautiful song with melodic chords. There will be high notes and low notes. Healing from trauma will make all of it a beautiful sound.

I have poured my heart out in this book because I want people to understand the cost of ignoring trauma wounds is massive. I urge you to take your mental health seriously and to invest in getting healed and getting whole emotionally, mentally, spiritually and even financially!

We were not created to suffer and live chaotic lives. Life is a beautiful song with melodic chords. There will be some high notes and there will be some low ones as well. It is up to us decide which part of the song we put on repeat. Will it be the beautiful melodic notes or the ones that were loud and chaotic sounding that we choose to remember? Healing from trauma will make all of it a beautiful sound.

While I shared quite a bit about trauma in the previous chapters, I want this chapter to drive home the fact that the choice to simply act as if nothing happened to you is foolish, especially if it was years ago and it keeps popping up in your mind or body. Again, traumatic events happen all the time to people and not all of them wound us. However, the real litmus test of knowing whether you have a trauma wound is the frequency that it appears and, most importantly, how it makes your nervous system and/or body feel when you think about it. One big question that therapists and clinicians ask their trauma survivors when they are in a session is "What is happening within you?" when the traumatic event is brought up. This is important because of the effect that trauma has on the nervous and sensory systems.

One thing is for certain when it comes to trauma healing—when we do not take action concerning the compounding stress and layers of trauma in our bodies, it will eventually escalate and lead to a "crash and burn" finale like nothing you have ever seen!

Judith Zackson, PhD, Founder and Clinical Director of Zackson Psychology Group shared some very interesting things about trauma. She stated that "Unresolved trauma occurs most commonly when rather than processing the traumatic event, the person tries to forget it and suppress it instead, by pushing it down into an internal 'black box' that only grows over time.

Dr. Jackson went on to say, "Unresolved trauma is an invisible illness. To others, you may seem fine, but in reality, you are stuck in the past, battling emotional and physical symptoms that make it challenging to live a quality life." I can say from experience that Dr. Jackson is 1,000% correct in her analysis of trauma.

CHOOSING HEALING: GETTING HELP AND GETTING WHOLE!

After looking back over my life and the amount of trauma that I have endured, I knew that God made sure that I not only survived the unrelenting amount of trauma that hit my life, but that I would heal enough to share my story and help thousands, if not millions, to heal as well!

As far as I can remember, my childhood was not terribly traumatic except for the things that I shared in the chapter on childhood trauma. One of the most traumatic things to date that I experienced as a child happened when someone did something that was inappropriate and was a clear violation of my innocence as a child. I am grateful that it was an isolated event and did not continue. This is why I probably was able to get over it fairly quickly and move on with my life without it affecting me mentally or emotionally.

Unfortunately, this is not the case with millions of other children as their cases are a lot more serious, which is why so many people (male and females) have mental scars from their childhood. Many will not talk about these experiences or even think about going to therapy. They mainly try and deal with what happened to them by trying to suppress the entire incident! So many have shared with me that they really do prefer "out of sight...out of mind" as their coping mechanism. To that I continue to say, "There is no way to uncross a bridge or un-sing a song!" Even if someone decides to deal with their trauma like this, it doesn't mean that it did not happen or will magically disappear from the history book of their life.

> There is no way to uncross a bridge or un-sing a song! Trauma will not magically disappear from the history book of your life.

As I stated in Chapter 4, "Relationship Trauma," most of my deepest trauma came about during my adult years and specifically after I got married at twenty-one. It has been a big trauma learning experience, and I am determined to use it to help others not make the same or similar mistakes!

When I married my husband, I had no idea that I was marrying someone with a long history of trauma that had affected him deeply. To make matters worse, he had never gone to therapy for any of it. So basically, even though I was insanely in love with him when we married, I was not prepared to take on the years of emotional wounding and hits that would come with this timeless love story! Even after we conceived and birthed three amazing sons, I was still feeling like the price tag for what I had endured in my relationship/marriage was WAY TOO HIGH!

As I look back, the years of emotional abuse I suffered is evidence of the importance of knowing your spouse's or partner's mental history! I am now advocating for new couples to not just concentrate on what their spouse's credit score is, but to ask about their mental health journey and to be quite inquisitive about how the healing is going. Ask the hard questions early to avoid getting some serious trauma wounds later on! It is crucial in this day and age to know if your spouse/partner has the mental capacity to carry you and whatever else may arise in the relationship.

***

It is beyond me why we shy away from asking our spouses and future spouses about their physical and mental health histories. Oh, I get it. "That's confidential information." This is inherently true, but after marrying and creating a covenant together, there is no more "single" goals, "single" problems or "single" anything (or least there should not be...) because now whatever happens to the family...affects every single person in the family! There should not be any more "single" battles, but whatever needs to be fought, must be fought together!

This book has been one huge history lesson about trauma and how it is affecting our society and, quite frankly, the world! There are so many aspects of trauma that most of us do not even realize. Keke Palmer shared in her book, *Master of Me: The Secret to Controlling Your Narrative*, that most people do not realize the impact of child-on-child sexual abuse and how traumatic that can be. She went on to explain how her "fame" was traumatic for her entire family because of the sudden wealth and dramatic life changes. The entire family ended up going to therapy!

This fact alone confirms what I mentioned in the very first chapter in this book and that TRAUMA looks different on everyone and in everyone's situation!

So, this is really what I want everyone to know about trauma:

- Trauma is real and should not be taken lightly
- Trauma can begin in the womb
- Trauma can destroy your relationship or marriage if you do not heal from your trauma wounds
- Trauma can and will affect the entire family unit
- Trauma looks different on everyone
- Trauma cannot be masked; unhealed trauma will eventually show up in some manner
- Trauma can show up in the workplace and affect a company's bottom-line
- Trauma can be the reason behind you anger issues or your depression (and many other issues as well)

- Trauma can affect your health and can cause serious health issues and contribute to early death if not managed
- Trauma can have a genetic component
- Trauma can be intergenerational, meaning it could have been passed down from your parents, grandparents or close relatives
- Trauma will not just fade away in the sunset; you must seek help with a qualified trauma-trained therapist or professional
- Trauma affects children in similar ways that it affects adults
- Trauma can show up from a financial crisis or disaster
- Trauma can show up from your church or spiritual experience
- Healing from trauma looks different for everyone; there is no specific timeline for someone to be fully healed

Here are several signs and indicators that a person is on a path to healing from trauma:

- A decrease in anxiety, feeling less depressed or fearful on a day-to-day basis
- Improved relationships and communication with other individuals
- An increase of trust and better relationship success
- An ability to connect with others on a deeper level
- Increased ability to cope with triggers and stress situations without feeling overwhelmed or affected

CHOOSING HEALING: GETTING HELP AND GETTING WHOLE!

- Increased self-awareness and understanding of one's emotions, thoughts, feelings and behavior
- A desire to reconnect with God and have a personal relationship with him
- Overall feeling a sense of closure or resolution about the traumatic event(s) and being able to move forward without dwelling on the past

It is important to keep in mind that healing from trauma is a gradual process and may involve some setbacks or challenges along the way. It is a journey that will ultimately require self-reflection, self-care and support from others.

I tell individuals all the time that it is perfectly normal to feel uncertain about your healing progress. It you begin to feel overwhelmed about having triggers and/or setbacks, it may be a sign that you need to seek guidance from a trauma-trained therapist, counselor or trauma-informed professional. These individuals are trained to help identify trauma wounds and find the appropriate path of treatment.

When looking at my own trauma journey, I knew that I had made significant strides in healing from trauma when my anger bouts were no longer disturbing my peace. I will be transparent in saying that for years my anger had held me captive. I knew that my trauma wounds were at the root of my anger issues. This is also one of the reasons that I felt I had to write this book. I am hoping that someone will be able to relate to my story and be encouraged at the fact that healing and hope is possible!

As I shared in the relationship trauma chapter, it was shortly after we married that I realized that my husband had some trauma wounds because of his behavior and mindset toward fidelity. I would soon come face-to-face with emotional scarring from infidelity, but I thought at the beginning that maybe it was just his adjustment from being single to the eternal commitment of marriage vows.

I remember the feeling the first time I confirmed that he had an extramarital affair. It was beyond traumatizing and a feeling that I wish I could erase from my heart and my mind. Unfortunately, it was not quite that easy, and the worst part about it was that it would continue for a few years into our marriage.

I felt the seeds of anger beginning to grow—first just a little and then as a rush of what I can only describe as an ocean of emotions. I would be having a good day until my husband came home and then it seemed like the minute I would see him, the anger would continue to grow similar to an outdoor campfire.

The episodes went from every few weeks to every few days as more and more trauma hit my life. I would try to taper it down when I was around my children, but every now and then, they would see what was supposed to be hidden trauma scars come alive! As the years passed, I knew that I needed help with the relationship trauma. I would make appointments with various therapists and would always cancel them a few days before.

In hindsight, I was only hindering my healing by overthinking the process and also by thinking that maybe I really did not need a therapist but only needed some time to pass. This could not be further from the truth. I have now come to realize that the saying, "Time heals," does not apply to trauma! Maybe the new saying should be, "Time doesn't heal unhealed trauma wounds—therapy does!"

So eventually I found a great therapist and she was able to help me begin the process of releasing the anger and finding my healing process. After healing from some of the anger, I was able to start the forgiveness portion. I am not sure if anyone else agrees, but I do not think it's possible to fully heal without first forgiving the person who wounded you. I further believe that it's possible to "forgive" a person, but your wounds still need time to heal! Some SuperSaints (people who are overly spiritual and in denial about practicality) will certainly disagree with my spiritual theory, and that's okay. As I have stated over and over again in this book, everyone's trauma healing journey looks different! Just remember this: healing is not to make it as if the events never happened, but to learn how to manage resulting symptoms, triggers and hurt.

As far as the anger goes, let me also add that being able to control your reactions and responses to those who are intentionally triggering you is likely to be one of the most powerful tools in your healing process. The most important thing to remember when going through your healing process is to not be so hard on yourself. Wounds do not heal overnight, and as much as we would like to forget some of the hurtful things that happened to us—the reality is it will take some time.

In closing, many have asked if it is even possible for me to heal from this massive amount of trauma that I have experienced. To that I say, first and foremost, there is NOTHING impossible with God! Luke 1:37 reads, "For with God, nothing shall be impossible."

I hold these TRUTHS to be self-evident, that God has never left me. Even in the darkest of hours, I still felt that he was rocking me as I wept even though I could not see him. People get to choose who they will call their creator or God, and I choose to believe in the only true and living God! There is just no way I would still be alive and would have survived the amount of trauma that I have and my family has if it was not for the grace of the Almighty God!

> "For with God, nothing shall be impossible." –Luke 1:37

But to answer the question of, "Is it possible to fully heal from trauma?" As I have attempted to explain in this book, everyone's trauma journey is unique. With trauma, some things heal, and some we just learn how to manage and cope. For many people, the path to healing begins with acknowledging the reality of their experiences and allowing themselves to feel the range of emotions that accompany trauma. I sincerely believe that if I were not somewhat healed, I would not have been able to write this book.

I can say with conviction that I will never fully heal on this side of creation from having to bury two of my children (my babies). I do not think that is even expected of parents who have had to do it. It's unnatural for parents to bury their children, so total healing is not the end goal…total peace and acceptance is! One thing I do know for certain though is through this entire process, I am gifted in the area of "Resilience."

Resilience helps to build skills to endure almost any hardship. While resilience will not make your problems go away, it will help you to move past them and to try and become a stronger, better version of yourself. When you strive to be a better version of yourself, you can help someone else heal from the devastating blows of trauma.

My prayer for you is this: I pray that you heal, thrive and live a long and fruitful life on this Earth.

Very sincerely,

Roxie
April 2025'

APPENDIX ONE
Trauma Treatment & Resources

Paths to healing from past trauma will require first and foremost—a made up mind! No one can heal past emotional trauma wounds for you. You must do the work that is needed.

There are a number of alternatives and therapeutic resources available currently to help with trauma healing. As the topic lands in more and more conversations as a result of people finally opening up about their individual experiences with trauma—we are starting to see more qualified, certified trauma-informed therapists and professionals offer their services so people can really get the help they need.

It is possible to overcome childhood and adult trauma. With the help of the right therapist, psychiatrist or qualified mental health professional, you can confront, heal and move on from the trauma by participating in therapies like the following:

> - EMDR (Eye Movement Desensitization and Reprocessing) – helps rewire the brain to move past the trauma. EMDR has proven in various studies to be an effective treatment for both trauma and PTSD (Post Traumatic Stress Disorder)
>
> - TRM (Trauma Resilience Model) – helps you learn how to handle distress so you are no longer stuck in the past

> TFCBT (Trauma Focused Cognitive-Behavioral Therapy) – focuses on the specific trauma and teaches you coping skills to deal with it appropriately

> Mindfulness Based Approaches and Cognitive Processing Therapy (CPT) are both highly effective in treating trauma.

> Dialectical Behavior Therapy (DBT) – focuses on teaching individuals skills to manage intense emotions, improve relationships, and cope with challenging situations

> Psychodynamic Therapy – a form of "talk therapy" that explores the unconscious mind, early life experiences, and their influence on current thoughts, feelings, and behaviors.

Again, there are many other modalities and/or treatment plans that may help an individual who is in need of healing from trauma. Research and explore other options as needed.

Cognitive restructuring is a core component of Cognitive Behavioral Therapy (CBT) that is vital in helping individuals identify and modify unhelpful or distorted thought patterns and beliefs related to trauma, which promotes more adaptive and balanced thinking.

There are a number of organizations that also help individuals who are dealing with trauma or who need support through counseling/therapy. When selecting a therapist or mental health professional to work with just remember that you are not obligated to continue in sessions if it appears to not be a good fit. Just continue searching until you feel safe in sharing so the treatment will be effective.

TRAUMA TREATMENT & RESOURCES

If you are struggling with your mental health after experiencing trauma, please reach out to any mental health facility, organization and if urgent, please call 9-1-1 so someone can help you right away!

Here are just a few places you can call if needed. Note: some of this contact information could have changed after the printing of this book.

- Crisis Text Line: Text HOME to 741741
- National Alliance of Trauma Recovery Centers
- Website: nationalallianceoftraumarecoverycenters.org
- National Suicide & Crisis Lifeline: 988
- Substance Abuse & Mental Health Services Administration (SAMHSA) National Helpline: 1-800-662-4357
- National Domestic Violence Hotline: 1-800-799-SAFE (7233)
- National Center for Trauma-Informed Care (NCTIC)
- National Alliance on Mental Illness (NAMI): 703-524-7600
- National Institute of Mental Health (NIMH)
- National Child Traumatic Stress Network (NCTSN): 310-235-2633
- National Center for Children Exposed to Violence: 203-785-5759
- The National Center for PTSD – 800-698-2411
- National Resource Center on Domestic Violence: 717-461-3939

ACKNOWLEDGMENTS

While I personally feel that my life has been one big question mark—I realize that God didn't create me to function as a question mark (?) but as a vessel! A human vessel is someone who is "willing" to be used by God for whatever purpose He has in mind. Therein lies the problem for most of us. We want God to use us, but we want the "resort" kind of assignments, the easy assignments that we can finish real quick. We want the ones that will not wound us so deeply that there seems to be no possibility of healing or end in sight! Do not wait for the easy ones to come because you will be wasting valuable time that can be better used living life to the fullest.

I sit often in my quiet place (whenever and wherever I can find one) and just ponder how a life without all of the trauma, tragedy, pain, hurt, disappointment, sadness, suffering and wounding would look. I am still asking God why I was handpicked for so much suffering and trauma. I am still waiting on answers as you read this. Although the answers have not appeared (or at least I am unsure if they have), He does continue to lead me down paths of healing, paths of calm and refreshing occasionally just so I realize that he is still walking with me. I continue to try and quiet my mind during these times but that is an ongoing challenge!

I really pray that my life and my testimony will give someone the "hope" and courage to keep going. I have concluded that some of life's biggest questions will not be answered on this side of glory. So do not waste the beautiful moments that are oh so valuable worrying about things that we cannot change. It is so crucial that we stop wasting time and find out early what our life's purpose is. Prior to writing this book, I had to repent before God for wasting valuable time by allowing so many humans to steal my joy, happiness and most importantly—my peace!

We say it all the time, "Life is short" but I really do not think that we understand the brevity of human life and why every moment must count. I never thought in a million years I would bury any of my children…that's the part I will never understand. Nevertheless, I am still thankful and grateful that we made some really golden, sweet memories while we were together.

So, I vow to use every unbelievable tragedy that has hit my life as a "ray of light" for people who may be in a dark place. We must stop holding onto our stories, our testimonies because we want to be "private". Besides, there is no such thing as privacy in 2025. Anything can be accessed either one way or another. It's the country we live in. We really do not have the right to remain silent anyway, after being blessed to still be here in the land of the living.

There will be plenty of time to be silent after our eyes close permanently…until then, please find someone to uplift, someone to encourage, someone to support, someone to cry with, someone to laugh with or just someone to sit with!

I tell you from experience, that "memories" is all you will have when a loved ones slips away suddenly. So invest time with the ones you love and trust. It's a reason why God created "family!" He knew that life would be too hard to live alone. Granted, some of our family members appear to be sent from the opposition (LOL) and you will know which ones are meant to be "once or twice" a year connections!

I am grateful for my family, my friends, acquaintances and even a few of my enemies. I know, some of us do not think we have enemies but that's where you are wrong. Jesus had a small, close-knitted group

ACKNOWLEDGMENTS

of friends/partners and as unbelievable as it seems, one of them turned on him. So if it can happen to Jesus...please know that we are no exception!

Some people have really been in my corner from day one. I played the piano as a young girl of eight or nine years old and always looked forward to getting my hair done for my recitals. It was the best feeling and I felt so beautiful inside and outside. I will be forever grateful to my two godmothers who did my hair. Maebelle Bryant and Hattie Kearney, you both are more valuable than silver or gold—thank you for loving me unconditionally!

After going to college, I met the sweetest, most caring human that I had ever known and we are still besties/super close friends now forty plus years later! Denise Bellinger McLean, you made me feel like I belonged at East Carolina University! Prior to meeting you, I felt misplaced and undeserving. Thank you for always making me feel special. Even though we only talk a few times a year now, it's as if we are sitting there in Garrett Hall on campus all over again when we do. I will always love you and thank God for allowing our paths to cross.

After getting married so young, I needed a marriage mentor terribly and before I knew it, one showed up by the name of Phyllis Moore. My sweet friend was always ready to pray for me, our marriage and our family at the drop of a hat! She was an angel then and she is definitely an angel now after passing in March of this year (2025). I will forever cherish our sisterhood and friendship forever.

Again, I am grateful for everyone who has ever supported me, expressed love towards me, and prayed for me. My siblings, my cousins, my friends, and more. I will never forget your kindness.

This project was a monster! It took me over two years to write this book because soooo much happened and I had to keep stopping for months at time. I am talking very serious family/life crises. I was still determined to share this story because I believe God had a purpose for my pain from the very beginning!

To one of the smartest, unbelievable editors in the whole wide world, Erin you are beyond amazing! Thank you for believing in me and my story! You went over and beyond the call of duty in order for this project to be completed. You will always hold a very special place in my heart! I went through about five people before finally running into my incredibly gifted book cover designer. Jerry, you are definitely a cut-above! Thank you for you ultra professionalism and kindness. I look forward to working on future projects together. I get so many compliments on the book cover. Mission accomplished!

In closing, if I forgot to thank you and you do not see your name in this book—no worries because you are inside my heart. Who knows though, I may be saving it for the next one!

Peace, Love & Unity Forever,
Roxie

TRAUMA QUOTES BY ROXIE

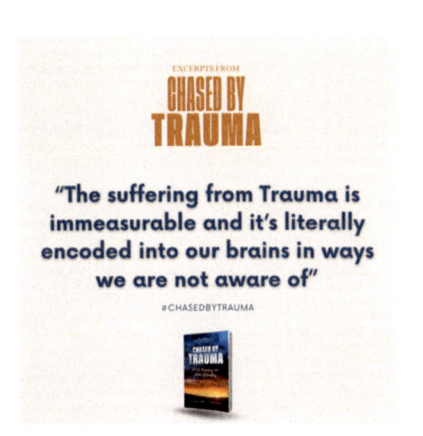

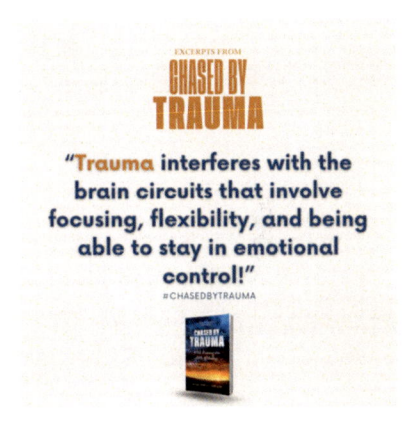

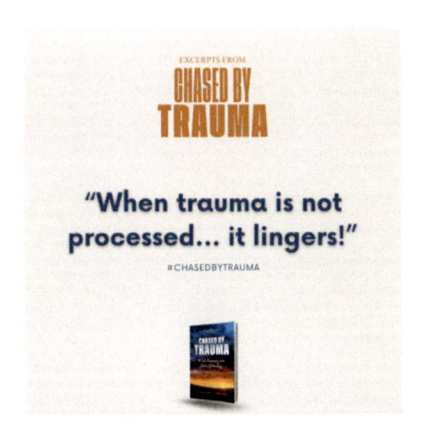

EXCERPTS FROM CHASED BY TRAUMA

"The suffering from Trauma is immeasurable and it's literally encoded into our brains in ways we are not aware of"

#CHASEDBYTRAUMA

EXCERPTS FROM CHASED BY TRAUMA

"Trauma interferes with the brain circuits that involve focusing, flexibility, and being able to stay in emotional control!"

#CHASEDBYTRAUMA

EXCERPTS FROM CHASED BY TRAUMA

Husbands- please know that you do not have to "go along" in order to "get along" just to have peace in your home! This can and will affect your mental health eventually!

#CHASEDBYTRAUMA

EXCERPTS FROM CHASED BY TRAUMA

"When trauma is not processed... it lingers!"

#CHASEDBYTRAUMA

NOTES

Chapter One: Trauma Looks Different on Everyone

1-National Council for Behavioral Health (name changed in 2021 to, National Council for Mental Wellbeing) n.d. How to Manage Trauma, https://www.thenationalcouncil.org/wp-content/uploads/2022/08/trauma-infographic.pdf

2-"When Trauma Gets Stuck in the Body," *Psychology Today*, assessed April 22, 2024, https://www.psychologytoday.com/us/blog/in-the-body/201910/when-trauma-gets-stuck-in-the-body

3-"Trauma Big and Small: Why It All Matters and How to Cope," *Psychology Today* (March 13, 2017), assessed November 18, 2024, https://www.michaelshouse.com/treatment-admissions

4-National Center for Biotechnology(n.d.) "Understanding the Impact of Trauma," assessed February 25, 2024, https://www.ncbi.nlm.gov/Books/NBK207191

Chapter Two: Childhood Trauma

1-Bessel van der Kolk, M.D. (2014). *The Body Keeps the Score: Brain, Mind, and Body in the Healing of Trauma*, assessed January 24, 2025, https://www.besselvankolk.com/about/biography

2- Perry, Bruce and Oprah Winfrey. *What Happened To You?*, (New York: Flatiron Books, 2021).

Chapter Four: Relationship Trauma

1-Associated Press, last updated 2016, "Diaper-wearing astronaut jailed in love triangle plot," *The Denver Post,* https://www.denverpost.com/2007/02/05/diaper-wearing-astronaut-jailed-in-love-triangle-plot

2 – "How To Heal From A Trauma Bond Relationship." All Points North, September 8, 2022, https://apn.com/resources/relationship-or-traumabond

Chapter Six: Understanding Intergenerational Trauma

1-Buque, Mariel, *Break the Cycle: A Guide To Healing Intergenerational Trauma.* (New York: Dutton, 2024).

2-"Generational Trauma: 13+ Effective Ways to Break The Cycles," (n.d.) assessed March 13, 2025, https://www.sandstonecare.com/blog/generational-trauma/

Chapter Seven: Spiritual Trauma a/k/a "Church Hurt" When the Blessing…Breaks Us

1-Lane, Timothy. *Healing Trauma God's Way.* Used by permission, (Illinois: 2021)

Chapter Eleven: Trauma in the Workplace

1-Mayo Clinic (n.d.) assessed August 10. 2023. Used by permission, https://mayoclinic.org/healthy-lifestyle/stress-management

ABOUT THE AUTHOR

Additional information about the author can be found on her website and social medial platforms. The following sites may be used:

Website: www.roxiedewittdawson.com
Instagram (IG) @roxiedewittdawson
Facebook (FB) @roxiedewittdawson

YouTube platform coming soon (May 2025)
Podcast/Live Events: Relationship Roundtable by Roxie

Other books available for order by the author (either on author's personal website or on Amazon)

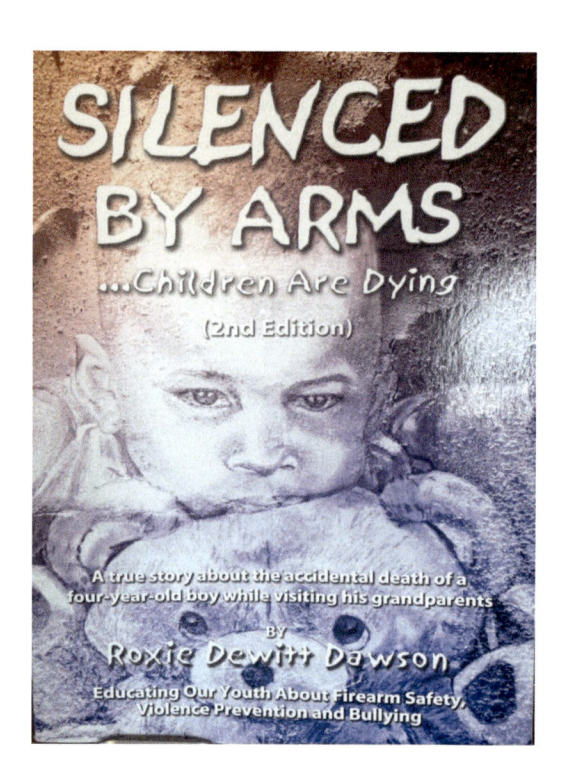